ONE ALMIGHTY

SS SUNNER

Copyright @2020 by (Surinder S. Sunner)

All rights reserved. No part of this book may be reproduced in any form or by any electronic or mechanical means, including information storage and retrieval systems, without permission in writing from the publisher, except by reviewers, who may quote brief passages in a review.

This publication contains the opinions and ideas of its author. It is intended to provide helpful and informative material on the subjects addressed in the publication. The author and publisher specifically disclaim all responsibility for any liability, loss or risk, personal or otherwise, which is incurred as a consequence, directly or indirectly, of the use and application of any of the contents of this book.

WORKBOOK PRESS LLC
187 E Warm Springs Rd,
Suite B285, Las Vegas, NV 89119, USA

Website: https://workbookpress.com/
Hotline: 1-888-818-4856
Email: admin@workbookpress.com

Ordering Information:
Quantity sales. Special discounts are available on quantity purchases by corporations, associations, and others. For details, contact the publisher at the address above.

ISBN-13:   978-1-952754-34-0 (Paperback Version)
                      978-1-952754-35-7 (Digital Version)
                      978-1-952754-47-0 (Hardback Version)

REV. DATE: 26/06/2020

ONE
ALMIGHTY

Almighty is one and only one. Two, three, four or more could be mighty, but not Almighty. Absolute truth is one and only one. Two, three, four or more could be truth but not Absolute truth.
Creator is one and only one, self-created is one and only one, immortal is one and only one, ever-present, who neither comes nor goes is one and only one.

Power not a person
Creator of five elements is a power, not a person. All five elements are power, not a person. Fire is power, not a person. Air is power, not a person. Water is power, not a person. Earth is power, not a person. Space is power not a person. Body need space, space do not need body. All five do not need person but person need all five. Without all five no creation is possible.

Master
Master is a teacher, yes, person can become a teacher. Person can become spiritual, but cannot become spirt. person can Conway spirituality, person can write scripture but not without word power. Words do not need a person, but person needs word power to become teacher. So, word is a power, word is master not a person. Words are the only way to write Almighty, creator.

SS SUNNER

1248 Mead Avenue Ventura CA 93004 USA
Email: ssunner@gmail.com Ph. 530 921 0097

ONE
ALMIGHTY

Almighty is one and only one.

Creator, self-created, is a power not a person. Creator God created elements for the creation. Creator was existing before all creation started breathing, every living creation needtobreathe, but Creator was there before air was created. No person can survive without breathing, Power that created air to breath, cannot be a person, Creator is a power. No one can survive without water except the Creator who created water. Creator who was self-created to create heat, air, water cannot be created. So the self-created creator is one and only one.

We can appreciate the creator, we can be thankful for God's grace, but without word power nobody can thank God. Word power is created by the creator to make us able to write scripture. Word power is the only way to appreciate One Almighty. Only way to get better is; reading, singing, listening and believing. Thank God, may God bless everyone.

The best part of every pastor or priest at a worship place is reading the Holy Book. If all of us start reading the Holy Book then we can all become pastors and priests to teach ourselves.

With best regards,

SS SUNNER

CONTENTS

Give it a shot	1
Zero	2
His Highness	3
Power	5
Only way	6
Universe	7
Grace	8
Truth	9
Creator	10
Spirituality	12
Great	13
Content	15
Absolute	17
Reasonable	19
Unseen	20
Trustworthy	21
Revealing	22
Unaccounted	23
Thanks	24
Scripture	25
Ultimate	27
Endless	29
Biggest	31
Priceless	32
Domicile	33
Satisfaction	34
Chanting Him	36
Confession	38
Doing it all	39
Mount	40
Divine	42
Self control	43
Takes care	44
Around the year	45
March	47
April	48

May	50
June	51
July	52
August	53
September	54
October	55
November	56
December	57
January	58
February	59
First Father	61
Step first	62
Step 2	63
Step 3	64
Step 4	65
Step 5	66
Step 6	67
Step 7	68
Step 8	69
Step 9	70
Grant me everlasting union with you, Lord, God Almighty!	71
All Power comes from the Lord, God Almighty. Let us Praise Him!	73
The Lord brings His devotees to His Everlasting Home!	76
Blessed is the man for whom the door of Eternity is opened!	79
Bless me, Lord, that I may be united with you eternally!	82
Lord, God, lead me to the sanctity of your Eternal Home!	84
Through devotion, you will be Blessed with His Grace.	86
Let us be exalted with God's Grace!	88
Bow at His feet to be united with Him.	90
The holy Eternal is the All-Perfect, Supreme Being!	93
Lord bring us to your eternal Home!	95
God grant us the Grace to follow your Path!	97
Bless us that we may reside in your Divine Mansion	102
Lord, lead us to your Path	105

May we find Grace through Prayer?	109
Fill your heart with Truth and He will bestow His grace	111
Reap what you Sow!	113
Only the Almighty is everlasting!	115
Find union through the acceptance of the Word!	117
Contemplate Truth and find union with the Lord!	120
The Lord God inspires all devotion.	122
God's Name, alone, will fill you with Grace.	124
Meditate on the Lord and find everlasting Joy.	127
The Lord God is always with us, let us Praise Him!	129
Lord God, let me not be deluded by materialism!	131
Through Devotion to God's Word, let the Truth blossom	133
May we be forever in His Grace!	135
Come brethren, let us Praise the Lord!	137
You are the Beloved Mighty Lord!	139
Blessed be the Name of the Lord	141
Never leave us Almighty God!	143
Grant us your Grace, Oh Lord!	145
Lord bring us to Your Devine Home!	147
Lord, God Almighty, be mine!	149
May I find True realization through His Grace!	151
Honor the holy Name, Lord God Almighty!	153
Freedom comes through God, alone!	154
With every breath may I Praise the Lord!	156
Contemplate the Lord	158
Meditate on the Lord	159
Nothing can be achieved without the Almighty	161
The Almighty is found through Grace	163
All happens through the Will of God	165
Live by the Teachings of Truth	167
Let God, alone, live within you!	169
God is both Mother and Father	171
God knows the Truth!	173
Without God, Life is nothing!	175

He, alone, is your Lord and Master 177
Be enlightened through Devotion 179
Taste the Joy of the lord 181
There will be no Doubt 183
The Lord God is in you! 185
Find your beauty in His Grace 186
Know God and Praise Him (2) 188
Know God and Praise Him 190
Enlighten us, so we will find our Heavenly home, Oh Lord! 191
Sing Choirs of heaven and Earth 192
Seek to know God through all that is good and true 194
The Supreme One 196
Running wrong way 197
Inspiring Prose & Poems 198

Give it a shot

Most of me might be worthless; it won't hurt you to read my thought.
I was digging in dark and deep; freezing, shivering, and sometimes hot.
Look like lazy and little bit loose; but believe me baby it means a lot.
Very different and hard to believe; thought is the same with brand new shot.
Somebody should have been upfront; somebody should have opened the naught.
You can cook up and twist the tale; someday surely you will get caught.
No thank you I don't ask anything; price or praise no mention not.
Highly obliged you will find me; pretty please read it, give it a shot.

Surinder Singh Sunner

Zero

Zero is the first phase;
nothing was there in the space.

No material nothing to eat,
air water or any treat.

No nothing no creation,
no movement and no station.

Almighty power a remote,
there was nothing ells to note.

First the heat was created,
than air was estimated.

Air became first charter,
mixed air produced water.

Water is the fifth aliment,
five created cent percent.

Earth is also made of five,
universe and total life.

His Highness

One, One and only One,
In earth, mars, moon or sun

The great, greater than great,
Only one is ultimate.

Yes, yes He is the one,
One, One and only One

Only one is immortal,
He plays, He is the ball.

Every play under His range,
He is changing, He is change.

Who is He? It does not matter,
His gender is rightly better.

Truthful and only true,
Oldest and brand new,

He is the future, he is now,
Wonderful, one can say wow.

He is consoling, He is sole,
He performs every role.

How big is He o man?
No one knows no one can.

No anomy, have no fear,
His position, crystal clear,

How He looks no one can say,
He is staying He is the stay.

He doesn't come, He doesn't go,
He is showing He is show.

He is grace He is God,
"His Highness" He is The Lord

Power

Let one talk about His power,
Let one take spiritual shower.

He is founder He is found,
He is never time bond.

Clockwise He will prevail,
Omnipresent never fail.

He was, He is, He will remain,
Rest of all is a big pain.

Only Way

Where is He, no one can guess,
His power, cannot asses.

You may reborn billion times
You may think trillion times

Goodness is one, one is GOD,
No one can become THE LORD.

No one knows His real might
Not even by keeping quite.

Greed cannot quench the thirst,
Chances are you will get worst

One may know a million trick,
Sickness will one day get sick.

Nothing, one can do at all,
Nothing else is immortal.

How? One can find the way,
What it takes and where to pay?

There is one and only way,
Where He keeps we have to stay.

Universe

Universe is in His order,
His kingdom, need no border.

Everything is His creation,
No guessing, no estimation.

Everyone is with his will,
Worthy, name fame or nil,

His creation good and bad,
Someone happy someone sad

One feeling, one is unable,
One feeling, one comfortable,

Within him if someone found,
He will still be running around.

Everything happens His way,
Nobody, nothing can say.

If man knows this clear and loud,
Then, nothing there to feel proud,

He is guarded He is Guard,
Explanation is too hard.

Grace

Someone sings spiritual song,
Appreciation never wrong,

His grace if someone feeling,
He is querying he is healing.

This is universal college,
If one acknowledge His knowledge.

Read write any scripture,
In scripture is His picture.

Sing song any melody,
All statues, His parody,

He is singing, if one feeling,
Sound like He is revealing.

True singer living creature,
True singer is true nature.

True singer can see too far,
True singer is super star.

True singer has lot to sing,
True singers are big ring.

He is giving away to all,
He is giving spring and fall.

We can't find Him, not at all
One can sing, and that is all.

Truth

True Lord Truth His name,
Different names, He is the same.

His love, and His blessing,
Keep getting without assessing.

Mighty giver is giving away
We just take and we don't pay

What we do to oblige lord
How we can realize God?

How someone can reach,
What wording and what speech.

How high is His Highness?
One can only think and guess.

Early morning one may think,
One may take a Holy drink.

One can think clear and deep,
Every one is when asleep.

Find truth your inside,
You can search and you can guide.

You can teach and you can learn.
Spirituality you can earn.

One can feel what he got,
All in you it can't be bought.

All is Him, Him everywhere,
All is Him here and there.

Creator

One can write Him in scripture,
Nobody can make His picture.

Creator you can't create,
Only one is ultimate.

Self created one power,
Nobody can build that tower.

Self created is only one,
Creation is all His fun.

Those who trust they prevail,
Otherwise certainly fail.

We should sing just His song,
Singing Him can't get wrong.

Singing, listening with full respect,
This is main trick in fact.

Singing Him with full belief,
Only way to get relief

We can get rid of sorrow,
Satisfaction we can borrow.

Faithfully if we can sing,
We can get spiritual wing.

Faithfully if we can learn,
We can make it we can earn.

Faithfully we can prevail,
Faithfully we can avail.

His Highness is only God,
His Highness is my Lord.

We can't reach His tower,
We can't know His power.

O lord you are so kind,
Always stay in every mind.

Spirituality

Spiritual bath is in His hand,
Spirituality is all His land.

Nobody can go his way,
Nobody have any say.

Everything is in His power.
He is taking He is shower.

If someone listen his teacher,
Certainly makes his future.

Teacher teaching in his tuition,
There is only one solution.

One should keep in one's mind,
One should prey the only kind.

He can give and we can take,
Everybody else is fake.

One and only one is Lord,
One and only one is God.

Great

Someone may live million years,
May be, one live billion years,

Everybody knows His name,
Too much publicity and fame,

Everyone may talk with him,
Everyone may walk with him.

If someone have good name,
Everyone knows his fame.

But, if he is not in His books,
If he is not in His looks,

He gets no number no lane,
What he does is all in vain.

He is just like insect,
He is no, nothing infect.

Unable He makes able,
One who just earns His label,

That one will shine bright,
He will feel mighty might

His Highness is so great,
No argue no debate.

One can listen one can tell,
What is haven what is hell,

Yes some people know a lot,
Listen to them, give it a shot,

Listen about all stars,
Listen about shining mars,

Listen about different sands,
How many waters and lands,

How many lamps and light,
Many dim and many bright.

Listening people digging deep,
One can listen one can keep.

Listening one can win the time,
Stitch in time saves nine.

Listener gets forever smile.
Keeping worry away a mile.

Content

One listening with concentration,
One listening with cogeneration,

Listener can become a priest,
Listener can get Holly feast.

Ordinary become the great,
We can't even estimate.

Listener learns meditation,
Gets behind estimation,

Someone who is listening Lord,
He can talk about God.

He can learn how to serve
He can see every curve,

Listening can make you able,
Reaching dedicated label,

Listener learns every theory
Listener joins religious jury,

Those who listen His Highness,
Their ability behind the guess,

His followers are all content,
Are happy hundred percent.

Listening can make you pure
All sickness could be cure,

Listener will be satisfied,
Listener can become a guide.

Listening makes you expert
Hurt no one, and don't get hurt.

His listener they get respect,
Their position is perfect.

If you listen you get in touch,
You observe very much.

By listening you get slow
You reduce wrong flow.

His listeners are all content,
They are happy cent percent.

Absolute

His Highness deserves salute,
His position absolute,

By trusting Him you get wise,
By trusting Him you can rise.

Trust is the only tale,
By trusting you never fail.

By trusting you know the Ocean,
Trustworthy all His motion,

Trust is the only locket,
Your trust is your Prophet.

Trust can create a ring,
You get voice you can sing.

You can see even unseen,
Trust can make you keen.

Everything becomes teachable
Everything becomes reachable.

Trusting Him you get oblige,
You know He is oversize.

Trust let you through the grief,
You can get rid of mischief.

Unprecedented is belief
Without belief you can't achieve.

Very hard to describe,
You can't trick, you can't bribe.

How big is His believer?
Too high highest achiever,

Nobody can tell his height,
How he shines how much bright.

If someone is trying to tell,
He is inviting big hell.

It is very hard to write,
True believer and his light,

True believer and his thinking
No one reach his eye blinking,

Only true believer trust
True believer has no rust.

Reasonable

One can wake up with trust,
One can make up with trust.

Faithfull determined mind,
Wiser wealthy wonder kind

Trust simply makes you best,
Anyway better then rest.

Trust is a worthy tool
Really reasonable rule

Dark bright day or night
Trust in God will guide you right.

You won't get hurt anywhere
Trust in God for sure takes care

Lifelong you will not fear
Trust in God will make it clear.

God can help you clean the rust
Only if you really trust

Unseen

No power can stop your way
No power can have any say.

Your trust will take you right
You will feel you're bright.

You will feel proud of trust
You will talk loud of trust.

When you really trust in God
Then you don't need any other Lord.

When you walking on right way
You don't look for any other way.

Unseen unborn self made one
If you have one, you are done.

If you trust He is in you
That is trust and that is true.

Religious religion all in one
If you trust this you are done.

This can happen with full trust
Full trust is really must.

Trustworthy

Full trust is higher level
Content and comfortable

Super status high feeling
That is upper level dealing

Upper family super relation
All beyond estimation

Trust is a special seed
Trust creates super breed

Trustworthy atmosphere
Neat clean crystal clear

If you trust you won't cry
Trust never makes you shy.

Faithfully you can achieve
Faithfully you can believe.

It require full trust
Full trust certainly must.

Revealing

God gives all good feeling,
God gives His true revealing

God bless who ever trust
You have to be worthy first.

We could be worth presiding
We could be able for guiding

Our good self we should find
Criticism we should not mind

Curtsy does create rule
Satisfaction is big tool

There are so many mars
Unaccounted little stars

How they are hanging there
Who knows who takes care?

We know only what we hear
Nothing true nothing to fear

Universe is a big tray
Unaccounted waterway

Lucky him who is correct
They are very few in fact.

Keeps us where He feels
God knows how to deal

Unaccounted

Unaccounted meditation
Unaccounted dedication

Unaccounted love creation
Unaccounted upper relation

Unaccounted way to prey
Too many logical ways

Too many title scripture
Unaccounted mix and mixture

Many teachers many guide
Still many unsatisfied

How many follow how many teach
Very hard to count each

Giving life as donation
Sacrificing for relation

Many dedicated brave
Too many in quite cave

Can't explain the nature
Can't explain creature

Thanks

Unaccounted foolish blind
Many miserable mud mind

Unaccounted dirty fame
Many leaving bad name

Too many can kill anyone
So cruel son of a gun

Unaccounted untrustworthy
Eating trash without allergy

Unaccounted backbiter
Too many meaningless fighters

It is hard to dig deep
As you sow, so shall you reap

You know what you doing God
Thanks, thanks, thanks my lord.

Scripture

Too many name and fame
Unreachable is this game.

Your light is too bright
Our vocabulary too tight

Nobody could find reality
Why to try and feel guilty

Still wording is only way
Without wording can't say

Wording is source of learning
Wording is the best earning.

With wording we stay in touch
With wording we try our luck

Who care who wrote the letter
By reading some can get better.

Wording letter one and all
All in one and that is all.

Who are you we cannot say
We just appreciate and prey.

The way you keep we should stay,
No other way anyway.

Dirt on some body part
Wash cleaning no big art

If so dirty our dress
Using soap cleaning mess

If so dirty one's mind
No soap of any kind.

Only way to clean sole
Scripture can do this role

We cannot clean mind
No Madison we can find.

Only God knows this phase
Could be fixed with His grace

Good, bad is not a talk
It depends how we walk.

What you sow, so you will reap
Marvelous or very cheep

With his grace we can improve
God behind every move

Ultimate

Courteous and good nature
That is just merciful pacer

That call is very small
Nothing to feel proud at all

Respectful listener loveable
This is really miner label

If you can clean your soul
This way you can play big role

All His grace, nothing is mine
My appearance very tiny

I get better if you want
Without you, no I can't

I am no nothing myself
I can do with your help

Creator and all creation
All united, is one nation

When this happens no one knows
You are showing you are show

I can't talk about your Highness
Someone might made a guess

His Highness you are too great
Beginning, final, ultimate

May be hundred thousand mars
Deep down million stars

No one knows who ever tried
No one makes it testified

No one can find the fact
You are acting you are act

You are greatest the great
You are the ultimate.

Endless

Every thinker every thought
Part of the single shot

When some river merges in ocean
River looses individual motion

Water canyons looking good
Searching ocean and they should

Big people powerful rich
Power comes from main switch

God given name and fame
He wants back you can't blame.

Endless praise endless talk
Endless journey endless walk

Endless count of creation
Endless grace and information

Endless power and position
Endless law and no petition

Universe is God gifted
Endless and is unlimited

Endless down and deep we look
He is shocking He is shuck

All this is His big creation
Just beyond estimation.

Nobody can check at all
Winter summer spring and fall

He created with His vision
Why He did He know the reason

His power bigger than big
We can't find we can't dig

If someone is really that big
Possibly then he can dig.

His Highness knows His height
Almighty knows His might.

With His grace we got it all
He knows who should be how tall.

Biggest

His capacity we can't learn
Giving away with no return

Giving away with no lack
Never ask anything back

Biggest donor biggest dome
Everything is in His home

Giving away biggest amount
That big no one can count

A lot of beggars' big boys
Big people get big toys.

No argue no dispute
His position absolute

Some beggars never say thanks
They get lost in their ranks.

God knows this all about
Where to rain and where to drought

Good bad is His assessing
We should take it as blessing.

Nothing comes without grace
He knows all number and phase

No one can be of His size
No one is wiser than wise.

He knows how to compensate
Good, bad, worse or great.

Priceless

Priceless is His position
No compare no competition

Priceless entrepreneur
Priceless stuff store

Those who do appreciate
Those ones are also great.

Priceless kingdom and rule
Priceless measure and tool

Priceless His helping hand
Priceless fertile land

Priceless His all device
Priceless without price

Priceless even His voice
Priceless is His advice.

Nobody can guess
His price Nobody is similar size.

Some people did try to say
Attribute they could not pay.

Domicile

What number then we should dial
Where is your domicile?

Where you sit and run empire
How you manage to acquire

Orchestra how you play
Who to sing and what to say

Lot of singer lot of song
Singing can never get wrong.

Universal one stage
Everyone is on same page

All singers singing in praise
Countless singers one stage

One creator only God
All music is for lord.

He is singing He is song
Nothing there can get wrong.

Our crop we can reap
We should live where He keeps.

Satisfaction

We should feel satisfied
Yes we have proper guide

Work hard whatever weather
Honest earning keep together.

We make the atmosphere
We can keep it clean clear.

We should keep concentrate
Just begin before too late.

Dedication is the tool
We can't play we can't fool

Full believe we should keep
May be it is dark and deep

We can win we can top
It depends on our adopt

If we can clean our thinking
Then we can be top ranking

Whole the world we can win
If we can win our own sin

Thank Mighty thank His might
One who absolutely right

Only one is right for ever
He can't be wrong no, never

One God made the earth,

It takes two to give one birth.

Man made total creation
Can't happen without relation,

Music song and singing knowledge
Teacher teaching many colleges

What we sow so we shall reap
Only our share we keep

Who will come and who should go
Entirely this is His show.

Trust God then no confusion
We can get rid of illusion

Everything we see illusion
Man made is key illusion.

Everything happen His way
No person with any say.

His game He is the player
His arena He takes care

He is watching every move
Where is He no one can prove?

With His grace we are rising
Who is He that is surprising?

God is builder there is no doubt
He knows how to mix grout.

Chanting Him

Truly this is His creation
All planets every nation

He was He is He will be
He handles His lock and key.

He knows what should be done
How bright should be the sun?

What He does He want to see.
He is doing all in free.

O my God O my lord
You are great I did absorbed

Chanting God again and again
Chanting as profession main

Chanting Him all day and night
Chanting Him we feeling right

God's Highness we can teach
But certainly cannot reach.

Yes we can sing His song
That is good nothing is wrong.

If we think we did find Him
Or we think we did kind Him

That is over estimation
Looking at a wrong station

Insect cannot fly
Certainly not too high

Some shows we cannot host
Yes we always like to boast.

Only if we get His grace
We can feel His next phase.

Confession

We cannot force our way
Curiously we just prey.

We can't even keep quite
Begging should not be a rite.

We can give up our possession
But we can't do it with passion

Even breath we don't possess
We might not like to confess.

One might be very wise
Nobody can force size

Even death you cannot force
Every life has due course.

Even then we all try
We try may not get by.

Doing it all

Day, night, spring and fall
His Highness doing it all

Space, water, air and heat
Entirely almighty treat

Countless creation birth
That is why He founded earth.

We get everything we earn
How we earn we have to learn.

How we did early or late
His Highness will compensate

Who is big and who is small
It does not matter at all.

His Highness He will take care
His judgment is good and fare

Mount

That is truth and truthful way
Nothing more that we could say.

Religiously we get this knowledge
Go to any religious college

Many teachers many tool
We can learn religious rule

There are many ways to learn
Many teachers do confirm

Many mars moon star
Many planets close and far

Countless divine countless devil
Countless are knowledge level.

Countless good countless bad
Countless happy countless sad

Nobody ever can count
Hard to conquer this mount

When we are in learning mood
Then we work on attitude

We can open many door
We can learn more and more.

Learning upper level action
We can find full satisfaction.

Work hard, you will achieve
We can do it if we believe

When we are self believer
Then we are highest achiever

When you are in upper phase
You will earn real praise

Work hard and keep awake
Learn not to do mistake

Yes we can clean our mind
Getting rid of conning kind

Working hard we can rise
Working hard we get wise.

Divine

When we are on that stage
Really upper level phase

When we learn how to guide
Then we find God inside.

That is highest level
Divine position where no devil

That is heavenly gate
That position ultimate.

True and truthful both are one
No one father no one son.

This level we can avail
Then we really prevail.

Self control

All this is a self control
We can always play this role.

We can always take advice
Teaching make you really rise

For sure we all can reach
But have to work on our speech

What we talking we should walk
What we walking we should talk.

No person could be perfect
May be scripture in fact

Only if we have His grace
We can win this human race.

Takes care

Space water heat and air
Even earth He takes care

We are all living with time
In good hands feeling fine

God knows wrong and right
All getting their due bite

All those who have full trust
They are clean have no rust.

Faithfully achieving height
Trust them they are all right

Around the year

Yes we are time bound;
still we like to run around.

Yes we are very lost;
finding home at any cost.

Help us God to find the way;
save us from going away.

We find out that we can run;
but running away is not a fun.

We should try to find The Great;
let us do it before too late.

Going wrong nothing we gain;
going wrong nothing but pain.

Running around here and there;
we can't make it anywhere.

Only God can show us the way;
only God where we can prey.

Without God we can't achieve;
hell with those who don't believe.

Some who say, he know it all;
one day he will face free fall.

We have only one salvation;
everything ells is intoxication.

We need only God's grace;
otherwise we can't show our face.

O Lord you are the home;
we can't get lost in your dome.

March

Think twice before you start;
thankful thinking is good art.

Yes we feel, we are growing;
getting big we are blowing.

Yes we feel we are Looming;
yes we feel that we are blooming.

That is all optical illusion;
unreal total confusion.

Spiritual people know the way;
what to think and what to say.

If we know we have some base;
why we join human race.

Rootless tree can get no fruit;
tree will die without the root.

Lucky those who understand;
all the noises are His band

We won't reach by going away;
stitch with grace the only way.

Thank him who tell this trick;
nothing wrong using this hitch.

April

When we feel this is mine;
when we feel human shine.

That means we are away;
certainly we lost the way.

What we see all is fake;
nothing real that we can take.

Willingly we are in dark;
what we see is not a park.

Unreal when we will choose;
we know that we will lose.

Son or spouse is all greed;
all is short living indeed.

Everlasting only one;
losing Him then where to run

Fake relationship is naught;
still everyone get caught.

If we don't have His grace;
for sure we lose the race.

He is only The ultimate;
no one could be alternate.

Some who really feel His power;
they enjoy holy shower.

All that glitters is not gold;
worldly things we cannot hold.

God is with us forever;
there is no substitution no never.

His presence if we feel,
we are healing and we will heal.

May

To the biggest we should bow,
all we see is all His show.

What He get is due respect,
everybody know this fact.

We are safe under His grace;
no devil can show its face.

We are safe if He is behind;
nobody can match His kind.

Very rich we are we feel;
His grace no one could steal.

What we have and what we are;
that is all His grace so for.

He is doing with His way;
His ruling we have to obey.

Some who are with Ultimate;
we can say they are the great.

He is there to show us way;
why we should then get away.

Why you bother why you cry;
He is with you don't feel shy.

When biggest big is at your side;
you don't need no more guide.

He is with you at your side;
that is enough to feel pride.

June

Those with no feeling of Lord;
those who walk away from God

They are feeling really hot,
they keep crying quite a lot.

To walk away is there choice;
no one other has any voice.

One who walk away from cool;
no one other, he is the fool.

Jumping in fire you will burn;
that is your choice to learn.

If you don't need His grace;
jumping into human race.

That is all up to you,
that is your company your crew.

Your rule and you are rebel;
that is self created trouble.

Yes it sounds very cheap; well,
as you sow so you reap.

Wrong way you running fast
can't reach at any cost.

Only one savior can save;
with Hs grace we can behave.

July

When we get tired of heat;
heat affecting heartbeat.

Where to go and where to hide;
when no guide or ride.

When we lost every tool;
either way looking for cool.

When we find we run in vain;
then we get heavenly rain.

Then we say o thank God;
and we feel grace of Lord.

We confess in the convention;
rain can't be human invention.

That is not a human power;
can't bring rain or shower.

Rain makes Earth fertile;
that is His trick and His style.

We want to know who does it all;
who brings spring and fall?

It depends how we find;
are we clear or dirty mind?

Who will find Him he is great;
same great and ultimate.

Nobody does know His might;
only we can read and write.

August

We don't know His all about?
He know His reason and route.

We think this is our show;
but who does it we don't know.

Can't be flower but we can smell;
all we do create a hell.

One day we all have to go;
death will end all devils show.

Where we go we do not know;
have to line up in one row.

As soon death will end our stay;
all ours will walk away.

One day we can be a hero;
time will come we will be zero.

We are known with what we shown;
even that will be blown.

Soul mate we think is must;
but can we define love and lust?

What we sow so we will reap;
if we are cheap we will creep.

If we find out God is there;
we will be content everywhere.

September

Frustration is not station;
no way could this be salvation.

We should try to know this fact;
our act really not an act.

His search was never right;
we can't lose the most bright.

We are searching far and near;
look inside o my dear.

O my mother we need help;
insider how can we develop?

Some people they can attach;
those who are of His batch.

His power we understand;
only when we stop our band.

End of me begin with He;
give up ego let pride flee.

With His mercy and His kind;
only way that one can find.

When somebody knows His
taste; after that all is waste.

Finding Him is a big art;
when you find then can't apart.

Then they feel fully content;
there is no other fulfillment.

October

What we deserve we can claim;
if we slip we take blame.

What we get we dig it all;
but nowhere heaven will fall.

When we lose His love and fear;
we get sick no one get near.

His blessing if we lose;
that we can choose.

All that what is so sweet;
nothing real but we can tweet.

If that is the revolution;
then hard to find other solution

No one listen you may cry;
you know you cannot get by.

We can't get with greedy looks;
what will happen is in books.

Luckily we understand;
every inch is His land.

Kindly give us a favor;
let us have a wisdom waver.

We would like to have a brake;
all we see is really fake.

Real part is your grace;
we are lost in human race.

November

It looks nice to be at home;
how nice is lord's dome.

How to praise who never leave;
can't count what they achieve.

It is great to be with great;
lucky those who subordinate.

Walking away we fell alone;
pale bloodless just a bone.

Walking away we are in trouble;
all fake whatever bubble.

Those who have God's grace;
they look good with charming face.

God's love and your respect;
that is the way that is the best

That is very strong side;
side with God as their guide.

Getting alone is a big shame;
you will live with your blame.

If we feel He is inside;
that is like a dream ride.

That is a glory of state;
that honor is ultimate.

December

After all that running around,
if His grace inside you found

You won't shiver even in cold,
you won't fell He will hold.

If you feel in His arm,
with that feeling you feel warm.

Walking away you were in pain,
wandering around and no gain.

You are the one who walk away,
welcome back you can stay.

He is yours if you feel,
no such wound which cannot heal.

This is your beginning and end,
you just cool down your trend.

You just prey you want to stay,
that is yours and you don't pay.

Only if you feel at home,
His entire kingdom is your dome.

For your mistakes don't feel shy,
pardon is privilege you can't buy.

All our blanks we can't fill,
all that depends on His will.

That is it you want to get,
in good hands you are all set.

January

You are back from heat and rain,
you found yourself once again.

Now you get some wise advise,
be humble don't feel too wise.

To give up ego we should learn,
greed and anger no concern.

We should get rid of our lust,
worldly attachment is not must.

Going right way we get praise,
we get promotion and get raise.

We get wise with His blessing;
we should give up our assessing.

Those who get there they are great,
those who are with ultimate.

Truthfulness is itself a goal,
truthfulness can play big role.

Cold and cool are different stages;
fall and spring are different phases.

All our thirst sure we can quench,
being with him inch by inch.

We can take this holly shower,
feel strong with his power.

Don't ever think of losing again,
everything ells is all in vain.

February

Yes our fruits are all in free,
but only for the grown up tree.

Yes we can become content,
if we stay with permanent.

We can be there with His grace,
content level is ultimate phase.

Whoever helped us he is saint,
prophet or priest why to complaint.

Beloved and lover are together,
then time to enjoy every weather.

We got back what we need,
seed become tree and tree gets seed.

Thankful dance and obliging song,
good feeling is never wrong.

When we know we got the best,
stick to that forget the rest.

Finally when we are stable,
then we don't need different label.

Savior served us with salvation;
no more traveling you got station.

We must sing millions of praise;
believe me this is the best wage.

God never need any return,
keep striate you got final turn.

One Almighty

Absolutely with His grace

We are here as human race

First Father

Powerhouse created heat, beginning of Creation Street.

The first aliment to be, first of five one could see.

Because of heat air blow, second aliment to show.

Air blew up everywhere, universe clean and fair.

Mix of air created water, water is itself starter.

Water is the first father, mother land needed it rather.

Heat air water and land, can shape up any sand.

Best creation human race, all other are second face.

HAPPY FATHER'S DAY sssunner

Step First

What a level o my mother
What a level o my brother.

I am so much satisfied
Feeling in heavenly ride

From the day I found Him
From the day I sound Him.

Feel like talking to Lord
Feel like walking with God

I feel fully content
This feeling is permanent

My mind now very slow
Got rid of usual blow

Now I have smooth mind
Somewhat supernatural kind

I am feeling so much great
This feeling is ultimate.

I feel singing inside
Something is ringing inside

If you trust talk to mind
If you trust you will find.

When everybody is content
Then no doubt no argument.

Step 2

Now I am talking to me
Inner position I can see

Keep always this feeling
You will see inside healing

No lose you only gain
Let Him do, why you pain

He can do it why I worry
Let Him do, why to hurry

He is doing, who is able
I should feel comfortable

Now I prey to stay with lord
I feel good to obey my lord

Step 3

You name anything lord have all,
Aliments, creation, play and ball

But it is up to God who will get
One who will get will be all set

Without grace we can't praise
And God's grace we can't chase

Very lucky who got praise inside
That person become good guide

That person can sing any song
All is right nothing is wrong

Lord and lords unique universe
God and God's blessing and curse

Step 4

Without truth we are helpless
But very few like to confess

Truth is reason of content man
Can we be truthful? Yes we can

Comfort of peace when we feeling
Then you feel like you are healing

Truthfully thankful to our master
Worldly wise and spiritually faster

Read spirituality watch scripture
You yourself can make your picture

Work on wording learn to talk
With graceful pride you can walk.

Step 5

Lucky those who find of truth
Five senses are kind of truth.

Don't you feel you are too hot
Keep control then you are smart

Keep your anger in control
Don't be lusty it mess-up soul

Attachment is not so bad
But over doing is very sad

Nothing bad if you feel proud
But no music should be too loud

Don't give up, control all five
Don't let them but you drive.

Believe me then you feel content
And this feeling is permanent.

Step 6

About The Lord we don't know much
Still we have to keep in touch.

We are helpless without His feeling,
One and only one revealing

His guidance is right and fair
Without Him can't reach anywhere

Without Him no one can save
Rough road of life He can pave

Keep blessing one and all
Your blessing is immortal

Through scripture we can learn
All aspects and all concern

Step 7

We just talk about satisfaction
But lust in us is big infection

True teacher can teach the way
If true order we can obey

Truth has no alternative
Man may be very creative

Mighty grace can cure disease
He can give us cool breeze

Who can give up all his pride
Scripture becomes his guide

When we talk about scripture
Life becomes a different picture

That level is content level
Truthful wise and very able

Step 8

With His blessings we run the race
All we get is all His grace

We can't do anything more
We are helpless to find any door

Some who run around a lot
One day for sure they get caught

No one should have any doubt
We can't find any other route

Only way is His way
His order we should obey

Dirt on mind makes us blind
But He cleans with His kind

Full faith is only way
No other wisdom no other say.

Step 9

We can't describe but we can talk
We can't reach Him but let us walk

Yes we know that we can't find
Not very possible but keep in mind

Full dedication with heart and soul
Serious and sincere can reach their goal

Let us try with absolute trust
We should do whatever is must

Only solution is holly scripture
Obey His order and stay in picture

We can be saint we can be priest
We can't catch Him but try at least.

Grant me everlasting union with you, Lord, God Almighty!

As a mother watches over her child from birth as it grows, so too the Master guides his disciples in love and devotion to the Lord. Blessed is the Master, the true Teacher, who grants us wisdom. As the crane circles the sky to protect and nourish her chicks, so also, the disciple is granted the love of the Lord, to hold and cherish, in his heart. All power is in the Lord. He cares for His devotees' honor, even through slander, from those who challenge and fight their beliefs. No one has any power but the Lord, God Almighty. All happens as He has ordained. Old age, death, disease, pain and curses will not bring torment unless it is sent by the Lord. Meditate on the Lord, God and even in your last moment, He will bring you peace. Joy and Bliss comes from God. Duality and evil is obliterated: Through prayer, with the Master's guidance, Union is possible. By the Grace of God, the devotee is granted union by touching the dust of his Master's feet. Seek the holy Teacher, who will confirm your dedication to the Lord. You will gain Blessings by repeating the holy Name of the Lord. Those free of duality and evil will have an enlightened heart.

They will know the compassion of the Lord, who, through His Grace, Praise Him and meditate on His holy Name. As a servant of the Lord, He has given me the whole world He created. The beauty of the Lord is in all creation. The Lord stays close by our side. The Un-limitable, Infinite Lord is here to shelter us. Praise the Lord, for He is Supreme Greatness. He is the life of the world, Master of the universe, the Creator. We must follow His Path and hold Him steadfast in our hearts. In holy company,

Praise the Lord, for His Divine Presence is the only medicine of the world. Peace comes from, and through, the Lord. From all sin and evil, we can be cleansed with His Divine elixir. Bathe in the holy Pool and all that is foul thinking and impure, will be washed away. The Lord has no equal. He is bountiful, He is the Sole Master of all. Praise Him and know the Joy that comes with devotion to His Divine Name.

Master of the universe, my Benevolent Father, grant me the Grace to lodge you, Lord, firmly in my heart. You created me, body and soul, save me from the clutches of death. Let me not be ignorant of your holy Word, like the evil reprobates and weak men, who are absorbed in filth and falsehood. You are a most gracious cherisher of those who seek your shelter, oh Lord. As your humble servant, I seek your charity, that I may become truly devoted to your Divine Word. Let my heart dance in devotion to you, for my mind and body belong to you. You are compassionate Lord, and you can shatter all suffering, hear my plea and listen to my prayer. Grant me everlasting union with you my Lord, God Almighty.

All Power comes from the Lord, God Almighty.
Let us Praise Him!

The Lord is all-pervasive, all-knowing, ever-present. He grants freedom, as He is the ship, raft and Pilot. He is the Master who grants all Grace and Blessings. The Lord, Himself, directs all His devotees. As the Merchant-Prince, He bestows all capitol that brings Joy to commerce. As His agents, He engages all His devotees. All profit and wealth is in Him, as we hold Him in our hearts and are protected from the tax collectors. They cannot harm us. Any other commerce is not shielded from suffering, when born of worldly materialism. Those whose commerce is in devotion to God will be granted His Grace. As a mother puts her hopes in her newborn son to grow into one who brings Joy and pleasure, so the Lord, God, holds His devotees in His arms to embrace His holy Word. Lord, God, comfort me and give me the Grace to hold you in my heart and be your honorable servant. All Joy comes through singing Praise to the lord. You know all things. All that happens is at your command, Lord. You are the Creator of all. Your ever-presence brings devotion to your Greatness. The slave who is bought at the marketplace is still the servant of God. He must meditate on the holy Name as he chops the grass and performs his daily chores. When the tiller, tills the soil with his whole heart, ploughing with honest effort to provide for his family, in the name of the Lord; The Lord will bless Him with the sustenance and enlightenment to know his God. In God's service, the merchant starts off with his lesion of horses, he earns his wealth but still remains a fervent devotee. He will find abundance in God. Those merchants who are only attached to worldly materialism are caught in duality and evil. Those who humbly serve God,

with the Master's guidance, will be liberated.

Those who are caught in illusion are lost in avarice and evil. Those who, although their load is heavy, serve the Lord, God, will be recognized by the Lord. Keep us close to you, Lord that I will cast away all thoughts of materialism and evil and Praise you with every breath. Monarchs and rulers serve man for their own gain. They impose fines, bonds and taxes to further their personal wealth. Blessed are those who remain steadfast in their devotion to the lord. They make no bargain to earn profit for this world only. Those who earn the Master's merit will profit by finding everlasting Joy.

Hunger for worldly pleasure is unquenchable. Devote your life to the Divine Master and you will be favored with his Grace. Lord, I seek only to know and see you. Those who have a heart that is filled with love of the Lord will be inspired and filled with Grace to become united with Him. Lord, though I have many demerits and have fallen many times in this life; Bless me with your compassion that I may find everlasting Joy in union with you. For you, Lord, are my Divine Savior. I am awe-struck by your Greatness. Lord, you are my Father, Mother, Brother, Sister and Friend. You know everything about me; when I have fallen and when I have sinned but still when I call to you in prayer, you listen and save me from death. When my mind has been attracted to riches and evil ways that are not of God, you have forgiven me. I was attracted to mansions, riches and worldly pleasure and forgot my Lord. Master, forgive my wrong-doing and give me the Grace to contemplate your holy Name. With your compassion, forgive me. All sinners can be saved with

the Grace of God.

The gift of life, limb, mouth and nose have been given to us. Water and grain to sustain us, clothing to cover us, together with other pleasures to enjoy. Let me never forget to Praise you and meditate on your holy Name. All power comes from the Lord, God Almighty, Let us Praise Him.

The Lord brings His devotees to His Everlasting Home!

All enlightenment comes from God. Through Divine essence all foulness is exposed and discarded. Understanding comes through meditating on the holy Name. The Divine Word obliterates worldly materialism, darkness and doubt are lifted. Those whose forehead is stamped with the Name of the Lord are His devotees. My brethren, by what means may God light up my life? For without sight, I will not know the Lord. Pray with me, holy brethren, that I may be granted the Divine nectar. Praise the Lord that I may listen well and hear His holy Name. The Lord, alone, is our true life's objective. For Joy comes from God, and my whole body and mind is absorbed in seeking such Blessings.

The Master has shown me the Way to the Lord. He guides me to trade sin for good merit and has adopted me as His. The Master has taken the sinners and though they are heavy as rocks, has taught them to swim across the ocean. For He is the Bestower of all merit and will guide us to cast away all sin and evil. Lord, redeem us that we may find the Way to peace in Thee. Open my ignorant, sleeping mind! With your guidance I will contemplate the Lord and know everlasting Joy. With God, as my true Friend, I chant hymns of Joy. This is my Prayer; Show mercy on me, oh Lord, as I hold you in my heart. I am no great scholar or disciple, but in my simplicity, I chant the Name of the Lord, over and over. Let the way my life is lead, through contemplation of the Lord, guide me safely across the ocean of the world, to your Divine Door. Those who are celibate and renounce all women and sit for hours and days on the steps

of a temple, or are great warriors who in their heroism, save the weak, will not come to know you without devotion. But I, in my childlike simplicity, hope that by repeating your Name, I will find liberation and peace. I may seem blind but I fix my sight in reliance on Thee and repeat your Name in meditation, over and over. I contemplate your Divinity and Greatness in the company of holy devotees. By listening to the Word of the Lord's inexpressible discourse, I Praise you in such holy company. My tongue will taste the Divine nectar and I will chant, as the slave of slaves, and meditate on your holy Name. The noblest of actions is in service to God's devotees. They are close to my heart, who teach me the Way of the holy Lord's discourse.

By good fortune, may I touch the dust of the feet of the holy brethren? May I fall in Love with the holy Name that such devotees are embodied with? As a mother is pleased to nurse her children. As a fish is happy to swim in clear water. So too, is the holy Preceptor pleased when the essence is offered to His disciples. Beloved Lord, Grant me union with such devotees of God, who have lifted away my sorrow and pain, by bringing the holy Word to me. At the sight of the calf, the cow is pleased. The woman is pleased at the sight of her beloved returning home safely. So too, God's devotees are pleased to sing Praise to the Lord. The lotus loves the gentle rain, the king is happy with his growing wealth. So God's devotees, fixed in their love of meditation and contemplation on the One, True, Supreme Being, God Almighty. As the simple working man is attached to his earnings, the true disciple is attached to the love of His Divine Master. As a beggar is pleased with his alms, the hungry man happy to enjoy his food; so the disciple is pleased with the sight

of his Master. Lord, grant me the sight of you, that my yearning to be enlightened will be fulfilled. With your Grace, fill my desire to cherish you, as the lovely wife who is over joyed when her Beloved appears. The suckling calf is delighted at the sight of the Dam (mother cow). No earthly love comes close to that which brings union with the Lord. Fruitful is the service of the Master, who guides the disciples to the Lord.

By whose touch is the Name of the Lord contemplated? By simply uttering His Name, all sin can be forgiven. So brothers, let us Praise the Name of the Lord and know His mercy. The Master will control the mind of all who contemplate the Lord. Day after day, chant Praise to the Lord. All falsehood and ego will be discarded and the radiance of the Lord will shine in your faces. Through the Grace of God, the Lord, Himself, showers freedom on His devotees and brings them to His everlasting Home.

Blessed is the man for whom the door of Eternity is opened

Quenching all worldly desire ends wandering of the mind. With this death, realization is possible. The medicine that kills the ego, awakens desire to know the Word. Through the holy Preceptor's Grace, real understanding of the Lord's Word is realized. Through good and holy deeds is the full understanding of the good-self ennobled by the Lord's Grace. Shed all ego and evil inclinations and you will never be alienated from the Lord. Those who are united with God from their birth and remain true to the holy Word will never be alienated. Those who lust after money for their reward are lost. Suppress your ego and know the Word of the Lord. The Lord is King and Judge. Never neglect Him. Why neglect the Lord over life? Why would you ever neglect the Ruler over all? Serve Him and make a sacrifice to the Lord's Name. The egotist, who in ignorance of God is involved in falsehood and duality, will perish. Those who follow His Path, please Him by Praising His holy Name. Those who have found merit in His holy Name and suppress all ego will know His realization.

How do I express my understanding of God? He is inexpressible, Almighty, Eternal and beyond our ability to evaluate. God is the holy Word. Through the holy Word comes all of His Greatness. Wherever the Master is, spontaneous congregations gather to Praise Him. Thus crushing all ego and evil. With devotion to God and meditation on His holy Name, He will be lodged in the mind and heart. That will bring enlightenment to enter His Divine Mansion, through His Grace.

The union of air, fire and water, has brought the world as created by the One, sole God. He is ever-present in every corner of the earth. His plan is incredible. His worth and abilities are impossible to express in simple words. Only those dedicated to Him will see Him and realize His true Greatness. By becoming united with the holy Word, you will be exalted with His Blessings.

Those absorbed in worldly materialism and earthly attachment cannot contemplate His qualities or seek enlightenment. Only those who are awakened to His holy Name are enlightened and will never sleep. Rare are they who follow His Path and find realization and His perfect endowment.

The self-absorbed, who have no piety, will never come to follow, or know, His Word. For they are deeply ensconced in the materialism and attachment of this world. Those who are blind to the Way of the Lord will never find liberation or closeness to the Lord, God. Devotion to God is the only Way to freedom. Rare are those who openly contemplate the Master's Word in this age. All are born in impurity and must find the Way to attain realization of the Lord. Through the Master's Guidance, and with His Grace, the mind will be opened to become absorbed in His holy Name.

By repeatedly contemplating His Name, you will cross the ocean of this world, and duality and ego will be drowned, by the Grace He bestows. The egotist who forgets the Lord, or those deluded will be wasted in a sea of suffering. Through Divine Grace, the holy Preceptor enjoins man in meditation to the Lord God. Such devotion brings faith to the mind.

Those who are devoted to the Lord become rich in their labor and will become enlightened through His Grace.

Brother, serve the Lord! Meditate on His Divine Name! Find reward in following the True Path! Find true understanding through Praising Him! Cast away all duality, ego and materialism. Don't be disturbed by the evil in those surrounding you, even friends, family, children or home. Seek, instead, holy brethren. Hold precious the Divine Name in your heart and be the rare one, who treasure's the Master's Word and is absorbed in Him. For there lies the real wealth, and through this devotion the inexhaustible, unending Bliss and Glory that opens the Divine Portal. Blessed is the man for whom the door of Eternity is opened.

Blessed me, Lord, that I may be united with you eternally!

The Master's guidance brings union with the Lord. With holy brethren, such union can be realized. Through fear of God, all fear and illusion of this world, is quashed. One who is absorbed in the fear of God can find true Joy. With the Lord firmly abiding in your heart, you will understand His amazing worth and Greatness. Through this realization, freedom, wisdom and purification is found. With Truth in the mind and heart, all your deeds and actions, will be good. Noble actions will be joined with the holy Word. With the Preceptor's guidance, holy service is rendered to God. Only the rare few will realize God's truth with the Master's inspiration. Through His Grace, love for God Almighty, is realized.

Where does enlightenment and truth come from? The holy disciples inspire the fire of desire. Through the Lord comes peace to the mind. Through the Lord, purity, holiness and sanctity is found. Through the Lord, union will come with devotion to the holy Word. Those who are without faith will remain in doubt and delusion. Through devotion to the Lord, God, comes relief from suffering. Through devotion to the Lord, comes peace and Truthful thinking. Through Supreme good fortune and fruitful lives, you will be Blessed with union. Those who do not know the Lord cannot find union with Him.

Through the Grace of God, love for His Name is inspired. Only those who find the holy Word will have fruitful lives. Spiritual peace and truthful thinking comes through the Lord's Blessings. Enlightenment

and Truth come with the fire of desire to know the Master. Peace, purity, holiness and sanctity come directly from the Lord. With the Master's guidance, union with the holy Word is attained. Without following His path, doubt and delusion, suffering and fear, remain. Through devotion and meditation, the One True vision of the lord eternal, comes to the faithful. God alone is the Bestowal, and with His Grace, union is found in the holy Word.

Through Him the mind is purified and truth lodges in the heart. The holy Word brings understanding of the One, Absolute, Eternal, Almighty God. Through good fortune and keeping holy company, Praise the Lord. Let your tongue never taste or utter falsehood or duality. Without the Word, your mind and body have no worth. Without devotion to the Name, only sorrow and tears will end life. Taste the Joy of the Lord and find the Grace of God in meditation of the holy Word. Keep your mind and heart upright to savor the holy Name. A vessel held upside down loses everything it was designed to hold. Holy is the vessel that thirsts for the Word and remains upright to savor each drop. Sing Praise to God's Name and lodge the Word firmly in your heart. Chant hymns to glorify the Master's Word. When God is pleased with those who are devoted and meditate with a pure heart, He will enlighten you to remain devoted. No false folly or capers will replace such devotion. Ego and ignorance will be cast away and freedom will be realized through the holy Word. Bless me Lord that I may never be alienated from you. Bless me Lord that I may be rendered pure. Bless me Lord that I may cast away all ego and evil. Bless me Lord that I may be united with you eternally.

Lord, God, lead me to the sanctity of your Eternal Home!

Cast away all ignorance by praising the Holy Name. For He can wash away all sin and suffering. Know that there is only One, Lord God Almighty. Worldly materialism may be sweet but will bring no Joy. In the darkness of ignorance there is no light. Ego brings only suffering. Be devoted to the Lord and you will be exalted. All that happens is His Will. There are consequences to all of our actions. With true devotion to the holy Name, you will never feel empty or alone.

We were born of the Father and Mother. Where did we come from? How did we get into this world? With fire and water, we were conceived. Why are we on this earth? The Lord counts all of our merits and demerits. We were created along with all other life, animals, birds, trees and fish. The thief steals from others, homes, shops, mansions, villages and towns. He is cautious as he returns home, peering around each corner as he clutches to his ill-gotten spoils. But he cannot conceal anything from the ever-watchful gaze of the Lord. Everywhere we roams on this earth, to shops, towns, market squares, rivers, oceans and mountains, our actions are recorded. We will be held accountable for all our deeds, good and bad.

The Merchant lives within us, and like the ocean is filled with water, we are filled with faults. But through His grace and compassion even the stone can float and swim to shore. The fire of sin and desire burns in the heart. Agony like a knife cuts the flesh. But in faith, if we Praise the Lord, we will find Joy and abide with Him in our hearts. We waste our nights with sleep and spend our days seeking food to please our hunger. But

fools that we are forget the precious Jewel that life is. If you never find faith in the holy Word, your life will be wasted and you will be filled with regret. Without devotion to the Lord, God, one searches for vast wealth, and leaves no time or place in his life for the Infinite Lord. But those who seek their fortune in the holy Word, will find wealth ever-lasting in union with God, the Almighty. Like a deer in the forest seeking to find herbs and roots to nourish himself, I will seek the Master's Grace and in His Name find true sustenance. That will reveal the illumination of His beauty.

To find the lord and happily meditate on Him is like the fish that happily swims through oceans. On the river banks and in all corners of the earth, the Lord is found. Behold the Lord, with open arms I embrace Him. Behold the Lord, though I am as low a creature as a serpent living beneath the soil, through devotion to the holy Word, I will be set free and all worldly fear will vanish. The home that joins together to sing hymns of Praise and acknowledges the Creator's Greatness in meditation, has no fear. For those abiding in such faith will find everlasting Joy. Everything is recorded and He will bestow the Grace to be united with Him eternally. Every home will receive the courier's packages, pray that the departed will be Blessed with union. Only God can bestow the gift of eternal union. By Him, with Him, and in Him, this union everlasting, takes away all worldly fear and doubt. Lodge Him in your heart, acknowledge His greatness through the holy Word. Purify your body and mind with God's Truth. Fix His Truth in your heart and mind and contemplate the holy Word every moment. Through the Master's guidance, inspiration of God's Truth is found. Through God's Grace, love for His Name is realized. God, I pray for the Grace to find peace, purity, holiness and sanctity forever in your Eternal Home.

Through devotion, you will be Blessed with His Grace.

Pride never leads anywhere. All power belongs to the Creator. All life and death is in His hands. Through devotion to the holy Name, His pleasure lies and union with Him will be granted through His grace. He is all-seeing, all-knowing and is our One, True, Almighty God. I place all my trust in you, oh Lord and ask that you grant me the Master's Guidance. No impurity is in those who place the Lord, God Almighty firmly in their hearts. With the Master's Guidance and Grace, they will know the holy Word. Those who abide by His holy word and follow His path will be exalted.

Those who share the holy Word with others will be granted Grace. All fear in this world is wiped away with the fear of God. Realization comes through the Teachings of the perfect Preceptor. Those who are born with the word and who Praise spontaneously are blessed. Those who are absorbed in worldly materialism and are egotistical will be bound by such falsehood in life and death. Through devotion to the Lord, day and night, all doubt vanishes and union with Him is found by those who cherish His Name with all their hearts. Freedom comes through devotion to the holy Word. The cycle of life and death is known by the true disciples of the Word. Through service to the master and devotion to God, the Master's Guidance is found. This Truth destroys the cycle of birth and death. Liberation is found through the Master's Guidance. The Lord, who loves the humble, will bestow all Blessing and Grace to see Him.

Avarice, greed and falsehood are rampant in this world. They carry the burden that leads only to dust and ashes. By listening to the teachings of the Master, and doing only good deeds, this will not affect His true Devotees. Slander, evil, lies and lust will leave others abandoned. Do not waste your life with such foal means in this world. No amount of earthly pleasure or accumulation of wealth can be taken with you to the next world. Only those who are ignorant of the Truth, savor such worldliness. Nothing comes close to the Greatness of the Almighty Name. Build a wall on a good solid foundation, otherwise, it will crumble and fall. Those who gather great wealth in blindness and greed, sharing nothing with others, will remain alone, and with ignorance, will find folly and suffering. All happens at God's Will. The lord is the Merchant-Prince and we are His agents, belonging body and mind to Him. He, alone can give and take life. The evils of this world will not bring harm to you and your household, if you keep the holy Name in your heart. The household of the blind man can easily be raided for his illusions cannot protect him. His family will yearn for the precious silver, gold and jewels. Once again, the blind man will attempt to gather ill-gotten goods, through evil deeds. Better to have the Jewel of the heart and the disciples of the mind, to bring Truth and faith in the Supreme Master. In blindness, never seek the company of hypocrites, for they will only increase your doubt. What good will falsehood and duality do? Leave all regrets and seek truth. Praise the Name of the Lord. Lodge the Lord firmly in your heart and know there is only One, True God and Savior. Ego only brings suffering. By following the true Path, fill your heart and mind with love of the Lord, and through devotion, you will be blessed with His Grace.

Let us be exalted with God's Grace!

The mind is totally absorbed with lust, wrath and worldly materialism. It is involved in attachment, greed, evil and falsehood. This is man's worth but those who cross the ocean are awakened. They learn to Praise the holy Word. Hail to Thee, oh Lord, holy Immaculate One. I am a sinner but you are the One true immaculate Name. Fire and water make a loud presence in the body but the tongue may utter a different pleasure.

Those who are false have no fear of God nor do they have any devotion. Suppression of all ego will bring devotion to the Word and take away death. With faith and meditation, perfection may be found. In falsehood and duality, worldly materialism is manifested. Those who truly believe in the Lord find a Blessed peace. Those who are cursed with doubt and duality have truly missed the boat. Blessed are all who Praise the Lord, God Almighty. By Praise to the Lord, true faith is realized. I do not doubt! I have found the elixir that has brought me Faith. Ego has died and the pure mind brings full knowledge of the Lord. By the Grace of God, I have been Blessed with the inspiration of knowing the Lord. Since the Lord has given me the Grace to see the inner self, I am more devoted. Through meditation and holy bathing and casting away all ego and pride, may I attain the highest absorption?

Our life is not eternal, however, by contemplating the Lord, God Almighty, we may come to His eternal shelter. All doubt vanishes through our love and contemplation of the Lord. The Lotus of the heart will bloom. The Teacher brings purity and self-discipline. By accepting the Lord, God, a higher and higher status is reached. By good fortune,

you will be aware of the Supreme Being. His Grace brings you Divine union, thus destroying all ego and doubt. The consequences of our deeds cannot be expunged. We do not know the future. He, alone knows all that happens. He has all Power. Let me contemplate your Name, for you are our One Supreme Being. All the consequences of our deeds cannot be eliminated. Only the Lord knows the future. All things happen at His Divine Will. No other being has any such power. I am not capable of knowing the extent of your Grace and Blessings. Ritual action, duties and all thoughts of caste discrimination, are known to Him. You are the ever-giving Supreme Bestowal. You are all-knowing, all-seeing, oh my Lord. The heart that is true and has the Lord firmly planted will be exalted through the Grace of God.

Bow at His feet to be united with Him.

The Name of the Lord, God Almighty, the Supreme Being, without fear or bitterness, comes Eternal life, realized by His Grace. Fear of God is good and holds a mighty weight. An egotist thinks he has understanding and voice, but without God he cannot move forward, unless the Lord, through Divine Grace, provides wisdom. Those who, with the fear of God, open their hearts, will cherish such wisdom. The fire of fear, in the self, will start a blaze. In fear of God, through His holy Word, devotion and faith will grow. Frivolous understanding with blindness and false actions is worthless. It has no meaning. Lodge the fear of God in your mind and all other fear is banished. For the Lord is the only true shelter for us. All that happens is through His Will. Fear would attack us, if it come from anywhere else, other than the Lord. Fear causes the mind to be perturbed. No one can live or die, sink or swim, without His Divine Will. All happens as the Creator ordains. You come or go in this world, or the next, at His Will. Those who are involved in violence, attachment, desire and pride, will have an overflowing hunger like a raging river. God's devotees, by fear of God, are bolstered. That fear is food and drink to them. This brings sustenance to the mind, awakening it. Others perish who look elsewhere to find peace. For all creation is His, as too, are all possessions. Let true understanding be your Mother. Dignity be your Father and Truth your brother. Accept these as your true relatives, to express and accept the power of the Divine. This is all beyond us, but with God lodged in our mind, as the In-Laws, and good deeds as our Betrothed, union with God is possible and Truth becomes our Progeny.

The body is made of air, fire and water and has a restless clever intelligence that feeds the many senses and the inner-conscience. Those who meditate on the Truth become enlightened and realize such Truth. He Alone is the Master of Truth that brings enlightenment. He opens the mind's ear to Pure hearing. The body that is molded with clay listens to the wind: So enlightened one, tell us who dies? With understanding, pride and ego, die! The precious Jewel that you seek on the river bank or in holy places is actually lying within yourself. The scholar, with his debates, does not realize the Truth s inside himself. Haunting spiritual ignorance will die when the Supreme One grants me vision. Bless me with enlightenment. Let me keep holy company that I may be devoted to the holy Name. Those who do not find the Truth and the Name will find only death's bonds. Let our true farming and commerce be to seek shelter in His Name. Evil and good deeds are both sacks full of seeds. Lust and wrath will destroy the mind, making it forgetful of the holy Name and only filled with impurity. Holy is the Master's teaching that fills the body and mind with Joy that brings realization of the Truth.

The water weed and the lotus grow differently. Those who have the Name firmly planted are like sweet sugarcane juice. By Divine Grace, in conjunction with reason, the body becomes a fortress where the senses unite with the Light. He alone judges. He is the Merchant who will grant exaltation with devotion to His Name. The body is born and dies! How does this come about? When is it born? How is it absorbed? Where is it bound? How is it liberated? How can it find eternal Light? With the Name in the heart, we are born. With His immortal Name born on our tongue. With the Mighty Name, one can transcend desire. By the

Divine, all are born and by the same order, they die. By the mind's order, desire is born and becomes absorbed. Only through the Master's order are such bonds broken.

By meditation on the Word and devotion to the Divine Name, is man liberated. The tree of life is the nest for many birds. Some are happy, others are sorrowful and are destroyed by their attachment. As the dawn breaks, they cast a glance toward the sky and their actions take them racing in many directions. But those with the Name in their hearts, look upon the earth as a pasture land and crush lust and wrath. Without the Name as your merchandise, the shop will be empty. By union with the Divine Master, the doors of ignorance will be flung open. Through good fortune comes union with the Preceptor. Joy in Truth is found by the Lord's devotees. Spontaneous inspiration comes to those whose heart and mind is dedicated to the Lord. I bow at your feet and beg for the Grace to find union with Him.

The Holy Eternal is the All-Perfect, Supreme Being!

Devotion to the holy Name drives away all enemies, ego, duality and doubt. Joyous are those who have found the True path. Through meditation and Praise of the holy Word, death is conquered. The Master guides us to know the Divine word. You cannot wash away your faults. Only through devotion to God and by His Grace, can you be cleansed. He, alone can pardon your sins. It is meaningless to seek worldly pleasure to banish suffering. Joy and suffering are the clothing we must wear. Sometimes it is wiser to say nothing when silence is the better choice. You can seek the Lord in all directions but look within yourself to truly find Him. The Supreme Almighty God, who created all the universe, will be cherished. His Name the Jewel that within your heart, become the lamp that lights your Path and home. Those who open their heart to Praise Him will find Truth and Bliss. Those who have no fear of God are destroyed by their pride and will fear retribution. Those who have no thought or regard for the Name, will wander the earth like ghosts. If you come into the world with the fear of God and bear Him always in mind, you will die with the fruit of that fear. If you just indulge in worldly pleasure, you will not leave this world enlightened. Grace from the Master brings the full enjoyment of Bliss in union with God, the Father. By His Grace you will find Bliss.

By His Grace discipline is attained. By His Grace Eternal Truth is found. Those who pull out their hair and drink foul water or eat what lowest evil soul rejects, will scatter their own excrement and have foul odor. They fear water, so instead they use ashes to wipe their hands. They waste all their parent's hard earnings and gifts. Their family is left with only sadness and suffering and no lamp is lit for them. They are castaways and wander around like a

lost herd, for they have become corrupt. God, alone gives and takes away life. Holy Water is the only way to find their Path through the churning ocean. Through prayer and worship can, the Divine Path, be found. The devotees that purify by bathing in holy water, from head to limb, will become pure. Those who remain un-kempt will be the Devil's disciples. Nothing good can come to them. Rain falls from the clouds bringing Joy for water is life-giving. Grains and sugarcane grow with the benefit of rains clouds. The cotton grows to save us from nakedness. The grass grows feeding cows that give us curd to churn and the ghee (butter) that we use to make a feast.

The Teacher is like the ocean. Devotion the river. Bathing brings enlightenment by cleansing us. What harm can cold bring to fire? How does the night over-shadow the sun? How will darkness obstruct the moon? How will caste discrimination affect the Purity of the air and water? What gift can be made to the earth when it is the source of all that grows. True honor is preserved by Himself. The Lord, holy and immaculate, will be Praised. We, who beg Truth of Him and Praise Him with our unending devotion, will by His holy decree, find Faith and enlightenment. You, Lord are the true Bestowal of all Grace. Bless us and bring us into union with you. May we be obedient to you? May we be absorbed in holy Truth? May we seek to learn the True Path from the Teacher? You know our minds and hearts. You, alone can Bless us with the holy Truth and free us from all illusion. I Praise you night and day that I may be called to your Eternal Mansion. May I celebrate your Divinity. May I feast with the celestial Name? By the Master's guidance, may I be Blessed. Divine Praise by the holy Word is proclaimed and spread. The holy Eternal is the All-Perfect, Everlasting Supreme Being.

Lord bring us to your eternal Home!

Those who are filled with false poison, pride and ego will be cast away to roam the earth. For they do not follow His Path. They are filled with lust and wrath. But those who are His devotees and humbly meditate every day and night, shedding all ego and doubt, will be exalted, by the holy Word. Their faces will be radiant. Those who rise in the early morning to Praise Him, as their Lord God and meditate, with their mind fully concentrating, will be Blessed. As the day moves on and the mind becomes divided and pre-occupied with survival, as we are cast out on the stormy ocean. Our hunger and thirst brings deep fear and suffering. The food we seek turns to dust and we become exhausted with the toils of the day and with Our eyes ready to close, we are inspired to meditate, out of the fear, as day becomes night. Holy bathing brings us closer to God and we seek the Lord and all of our desire becomes Love for Him. The wealth of our Infinite God brings good fortune and this Truth is realized through devotion.

With God in my heart, who else will I need? The thief of selfishness will not harden the hearts of those who are devoted to Truth. With ego and doubt gone, the Truth is found in prayer. The Master will bless His servant with the genuine coins needed to enter the Divine Door. Those with the holy Name firmly lodged in their hearts will be filled beyond imagination with worldly treasure. With the guidance of the Teacher true merit is found. Again the early morning comes and those who awaken with the Joy of God in their hearts are spiritually inspired. With holy brethren, Praise the Name day and night. One becomes Blessed and filled

with good fortune. Just as the goldsmith rubs the gold and polishes it to a bright shining finish, so too the Divine Jeweler showers His devotees with Grace and they shine with Love, Truth and goodness. Air is the Supreme Master. Water the precursor. The earth the Mother. Night and day the playground of the world. Good and evil are judged in the Divine presence. Some by their good deeds are brought in to His holy company. Others cast away.

Those who have meditated on the Name, and have struggled, will be liberated. Their faces radiant. Of God is the one true nourishment that brings good living and true Joy. In this fortress of Truth, make your home. By the Grace of God, the ecstasy of His holy name is obtained. Falsehood and ego will not bring you to the Divine Mansion. By listening to the holy Truth, day and night, and by realization, you will gain entry to His Eternal Home.

God grant us the Grace to follow your Path!

Should I have fine garments of fire, a house built of snow and if I were to eat iron, what good would I be? If I could swallow all suffering and move the earth. If I could weigh the heavens on a scale with pennyweights and try to expand beyond measure or try to lead all creation by the nose with great power: It would still be nothing by comparison to how great the Lord is. He grants us whatever His Will decides. I pray for His grace to give me the inspiration to Praise His name. The tongue is not satisfied with idle chatter nor the ears with hearing it and the eyes never satiated with fake beholding. Those who are full of desire are never satisfied, as such hunger is only filled with Divine praise. Only God is True and real, all else is useless. Without the Lord and Truth all turns to dust and such dust has no eternal worth.

The Divine mansion is not attained through falsehood, greed and delusion. The fire of desire, when fueled with the Divine Word, can be reached. The Master is the tree of contentment and fortitude. The flower is righteousness and the fruit enlightenment. Through Joy that is found only in the Lord, the tree remains ever-green. Through meditation the fruit is ripened. With the love and Joy of the Lord, it is consumed. Acts of selfless charity and kind deeds done in His Name are counted. The golden tree with leaves of pearls, diamonds and rubies as the flowers and other precious jewels as the fruit, when shared in homily with holy brethren and all Truth seekers, becomes Joy in the hearts of the devotees. This good fortune will be recorded and the brethren will be bathe in the Master's holy waters. Through God's Grace they will be saved from the

rivers of fire, violence, attachment, avarice and wrath. Desire and evil will be destroyed. There will be no regrets for the faithful. For the falsehood and lack of reality of this world will be washed away by Truth and God's ordinance for His devotees.

Firmly lodge the Lord in your mind. Devote your every moment to Him and through His Grace, you will be enlightened. In holy Truth, become absorbed. In mind and heart hold the Lord. From all poison and bitter fruits, you will be saved. You will earn merit and be protected from all that is corrupt. Through the Master's guidance, you will follow His path and through the Divine Word, you will reside in His Eternal Home. Though you may be able to charm a scorpion, this does not give you the power to grasp snakes. Should an egotist challenge a believer, by Divine justice, he will be crushed. The Lord God Almighty determines the Truth. The goldsmith tests his own skill. The wise physician knows the ailment and the cure. The wayfarer or cordial guest knows the limits of his host. A truthful mediator is not prone to temptation but adheres to justice. Night and day meditate and obey God's Will. You will receive the loving affection of the Lord. You will become radiant through your devotion to His holy Name. To live without devotion to the Name is a curse. Those who live with the Truth of the holy Word will be exalted. Praise the Lord and seek His grace to follow his Path. God, grant me the Grace to follow your Path.

Lord, who is all powerful, Grant us union with you.

The crop is reaped when it is ripe. Husks tossed aside, the chaff crushed and the grain winnowed (cleaned). The sugarcane is cut, bound

and stacked like pillars, by strong men. The juice is boiled and the husks are burned. Those who are oblivious to death are filled with desire. They think they are superior to others. They are materialistic and worldly. Without gratitude, they are false and pay no respect to the Master. Those who bare the holy Name on their tongue and Praise Him, the Divine Master will take account of, and record, their devotion. How does deep water affect the fish or high altitude the birds or cold the stones? What good is a hermaphrodite to a wife? Will the deaf hear you read scripture or the blind see with a thousand lights? The farmer's herd cannot eat gold. Nor can iron, no matter how it is molded, feel soft like cotton. So it is, that time is wasted on the ignorant who have no will to change.

Will the blacksmith, with his fire, fuse broken metals? Should the husband abandon his wife or bare offspring to bolster his marriage? When the king or ruler makes demands, will a tax satisfy him? Will hunger be averted by food alone? Will rain and overflowing rivers cure famine? In love, understanding and communication brings reunion. Acceptance of Truth, in Holy Scripture, heals. Righteousness and reconciliation brings life. Some times the stubborn one needs a slap to open their eyes. The Lord has given birth to all creation and He thinks of all. He judges the true and the fake. He will cast away the fake to roam aimlessly. He will give shelter to those who hold the holy Word in their hearts. Those who are devoted to the holy Master will be shown Grace and will live in the Divine home.

There is only One, True God. Only He is eternal. Neither the sun, moon, stars, continents, oceans nor air, are constant. Only the Lord,

God Almighty. All hope comes from Him. He is the sole Creator, the One True and eternal Being. The birds need no gold or wealth, in hope of finding food or water. He provides for them. The Lord alone knows what is stamped on your forehead. Those who are guided by the Master's Will, discarding all ego and falsehood, will be enlightened. Those who contemplate the Truth will abide in Life eternal through the holy Word. The egotist who lives in illusion will abide in filth and never know the Lord. Alienated from the True Path, they will not find Grace. The goldsmith will tests the precious metal and will distinguish between genuine and fake. He may feed tigers, hawks, falcons and eagles with vegetables or turn a vegetarian to a carnivore. This is in His power. He is almighty. He can change the river's course or turn the fertile valley to an ocean. He can make a worm into a king or reduce massive holdings to ashes. He can keep the breathless living. Some He will make carnivores, some vegetarians, some will dine on a multitude of delicacies while others eat only dust. With Him as the Provider, none need to starve. With good fortune you may be endowed and obey the Lord. Without devotion, no joy or peace is found.

Meditate on the holy Name and your life will not be wasted. Praise the holy Name and absorb yourself in His Truth. For without devotion, no Joy or Peace is found. You will roam the earth finding only fake merchandise and making false gains. Some, who worship through music and hymns of Praise, please the Lord. Some, who bathe in holy Ponds, please the Lord. Also those who read scripture and become disciples, please Him. Some, He will make rulers, others will become defenders and have their heads severed from their bodies. Some will travel the earth,

and return home with great Knowledge. All is done with His knowledge. Those who are devoted to you and follow your path will be Blessed. You are the source of all good things. Our movements, our life, our death, all is known to you. With your guidance, may we follow the True Path and be Blessed with eternal life. Through devotion, all illusion will be lifted. May we always be devoted to the holy Name. The egotist will wallow in evil and find no rest. The truthful, obeying your Will, are called to the eternal Mansion. May we be reckoned holy through absorption in the Master's Truth. Bless us with the Grace that brings everlasting Joy. Lord, you are all powerful, grant us union with you.

Bless us that we may reside in your Divine Mansion

Man meditates on the Lord's Name. With contemplation on the holy Name, he finds Joy, through the Lord's Blessings. Through body and mind, union with the Creator is possible. Union and separation is made possible by Him, Alone. Worldly pleasure and ignorance bring only suffering. Indulgence in pleasure and sins brings maladies. From pleasure, sorrow of separation and suffering engulfs the ignorant person. He will be soaked in calculations and disputes. Only the holy Preceptor can settle disputes and bring peace. He settles all and He knows all. All is in His power and man can not accomplish anything without Him. One who acquires money or fortune through false pretenses and imparts such evil ways to others, will be lost and robbed of all goodness. So too, will all his associates. One who follows the Lord's Path and with a truthful tongue speaks the holy Name, will be stripped of all impurity. One who guides others to the Path of the Lord will be cleansed of all impurity.

Bathing alone will not rid him of filth. However, by increasingly meditating on the holy Name and remaining in the holy Preceptor's Pond, he will receive the gift of devotion and light. With a true and pure heart, Praise the Lord's Name. Those who are ignorant, full of pride will be judged. Learn the holy Name through contemplation of the Master's teachings. Realize the Name, garner your wealth in the holy Name and the treasure of Faith will become yours. Through contemplation of the holy Name is one judged pure, at the time they come to enter the Divine Home. Those who are enlightened have true wealth. The whole world comes to do business, let it be done with Him. Let your church be built

of compassion, your prayers filled with sincerity. Let scripture teach you honesty and bring you fair earnings. Be modest, noble and charitable. Let Truth be your teacher and all good deeds, your faith and prayer. Do what pleases the Lord and your honor will be justified.

Never take what belongs to another, this is evil. The Lord will forgive sin but not if your wealth is retained from evil commerce and falsehood. Just by talking, Truth is not attained. From good and decent acts, comes forgiveness. Forbidden foods are not deemed lawful just because the finest seasoning and herbs are used. The reward for falsehood is just that, false. The prayers of those with Faith and Truth are real. Let truth be your first prayer. Followed that by a prayer for good and legitimate earnings. Next pray for healing of the universe, a pure heart and mind and Praise for the Lord God.

Affirm your Faith with noble deeds. Hypocrites will not find peace. Some merchants deal their wears and jewel with truth and honesty, others sell only fake commodities. By the Grace of God, you will discover the real treasure of Truth in the house of Jewels. Blind hypocrites and egotists are ignorant of the Truth. They deal in evil and duality and find only suffering and destruction. There is only One Creator. Pray for His Guidance, whether you are a pauper or a prince. The holy Name is the only true wealth. Nothing else matters. All that is done in the Name of the Most High will be exalted.

Follow the True Path. Open your heart to love the Lord. Seek the Master's guidance, and through His grace, the illusion of death and life will banish. Be obedient to the Lord's Will. The faithful will know His

compassion. As you discard lust, wealth, falsehood, slander, materialism and pride, and cast away all attachments, you will attain the Supreme Immaculate Being, through His Grace. With His guidance in the holy Word, you will become absorbed in the holy Name Divine. Nothing else lasts. Kings, beggars, markets, town and countries will all disappear. In the Might of the Lord, all things are found. Fountains and streams that flow with milk and butter. A world with mounds of sugar delighting hearts. Gold and silver encrusted with diamonds and rubies all around. But none of this has a minute particle of the luxury that abounds in the hearts filled with Joy that praises the One true God. Whether my life is filled with all the luxurious fruits and grandeur of the world or afflicted with the struggles of hunger and thirst, I will contemplate the Lord. In meditation, I will find my heart filled with Joy. Never let me, for an instant, be forgetful of the holy Name. To live without the Lord, brings only ruin and delusion. Knowing both paths, let me follow the true Path, discarding all evil, rejecting illegitimate gains, all worldly materialism, falsehood, ego and desire. Fine food, elegant clothing, voluptuous pleasures, soft beds and mansions with servants, will not bring true Joy and Bliss. Only by truthful living and love of the holy Word will I find the love of the Lord for eternity. For He is my righteous ruler. May we be Blessed to live in His Divine mansion eternally.

Lord, lead us to your Path

The fire of desire in man is not satisfied in this world of doubt. The cycle of birth and death is all around. Without the guidance of the holy Preceptor, no illusion or doubt can be shattered. No exhaustive rituals will bring comfort and light. Meditate on the Wisdom of the Master and with His Grace, you will find the Truth that brings Joy and fulfillment. Those who devoutly meditate on the holy Word bring peace and liberation to all of their brethren. Blessed is the Mother that bore such devout disciples, for they hold the Lord steadfast in their hearts. Their reputation and Wisdom is held in high esteem. Without eyes to see, ears to hear, feet to move, hands to act or a tongue to speak, there is no Joy. For the faculties of sight, hearing and knowing alone, do not bring Joy. Without devotion, one is blind, limp, deaf and motionless. They can not run to the arms of the Lord. They must first seek to serve at the feet of Him, open their eyes to devotion and their hearts to the Love of Him.

The wise one will find union with the Lord. They will not be affected by any falsehood, also created by the Lord, such as ego and duality. Greed and avarice are also part of His creation. All things happen at the Creators Will. To some He will show Grace and grant them union with Him. Seek the Master's Guidance, in holy company find inspiration. Become absorbed in the holy Name, through devotion to the Lord. No amount of ritual, rigor or bathing will render me clean and rid of filth. Such darkness is not abolished by washing your clothing repeatedly. True piety is found in shedding all ego and falsehood, through the contemplation of the holy Word. Although man may wash himself and his clothing and

be disciplined, if he is unaware of the impurity within, he will remain blind and deluded. He will stay in the trap of ego and duality. Only through the Master's guidance, will ego be shattered. Meditate on the Lord. Contemplate His Name. Be devoted to His holy Name and with His Grace, you will fine Joy. In ignorance, if one remains involved in worldly pleasure, only suffering and pain will result. Such indulgence in sin brings separation and suffering. This malady causes the ignorant to engage in disputes and without the holy Preceptor's power, such disputes will never be settled. All happens at the Will of the Creator. Gains that come from false means will rob you, your family and associates of any goodness. Those who have truth in their heart, use a truthful tongue to acknowledge the holy Name. They follow, and guide others, on the Path of the Lord. They will become pure. Bathing in the pond of the Lord, will lead to removing all filth. This Sacred Pond is the holy Preceptor. Gather your tribe together and meditate often on the Divine Name. Inspire others to come, welcoming them and guiding them to reach awareness, through the Grace of God. There are some who live in simplicity, eating herbs and vegetables, in the forest. Others, in fancy pilfered clothing, with excessive desire, waste their lives. They have no anchor, no home. They roam the earth aimlessly. They will not find peace. The humble servant of the Lord, who has the holy Word firmly planted in his heart, will be emancipated. They will be Blessed with everlasting Joy and peace.

Humbly we seek your Blessings!

I will be devoted to the holy Preceptor day and night. I will contemplate the Lord discarding all ego and falsehood. Lord, I seek your

shelter. I Praise you with sweet words and beg your Blessings so I might find refuge in union with you. You are my One, True Friend. You, alone bring peace to my mind. I will search all corners of the earth to know your truth. I am your servant and only through good deeds and actions, I will be saved with your Grace. I lay myself before you, as no other can help me. Without you, oh kind and compassionate Lord, I am nothing. No other being is Great like you. No other can grant me forgiveness and Joy. No other can rid me of my pain and suffering. The state of my self, I lay at your feet and pray you will Bless me. The seeker of truth, pleases Him. You, Lord are the cherisher of the humble, Benevolent Savior of the fallen. You are the most compassionate Divine Being, Creator of the holy Name. No one knows or understands your full worth or value. I meditate night and day and beg at your feet for your guidance. Dear Lord Supreme, let my heart be your abode. Grant me your Grace. Forgive any sin I am guilty of. Blessed is the man in whom the Lord has found union. In your Name, may I find my life's true Path. Guide me so I will follow your Will. May I never covet more than you have granted me.

In holy company, I chant your Praise. There is not any other place that I can bring my sorrow and pray for relief and understanding. You, Alone bestow all Blessings. I fall at your feet and beseech you to hear your servant's fervent prayer. There are many stages of life. First, man is born of the Mother's womb and with her milk is nurtured. This child grows to know his parents, siblings and relatives. He finds love in his life and then enjoys the delicacies prepared for his table. He learns to overcome lust and aviaries. Gathers his wealth and fortune and settles in his home. His bodily strength begins to wane, hair turns grey and soon this life ends. His beloved, together with

family and friends, mourn his departure from this life. The swan has flown to a new Path, in the hereafter. Let us not ignore your teachings. At 10 the boy is called a man. At 20 he arrives at the full blossom of youth. At 30 his manly peak is reached. At 40 his manhood finds maturity. At 50 his steps may falter. At 60 comes the age of maturity. At 70 his senses start to wane. By 80 and 90 he becomes feeble and frail. It is time to find rest. The Supreme Creator knows all things. With devotion to His holy Name throughout your life, you will not die. The holy Immaculate Lord, will bring His devotees into His Divine home. With a sincere heart, meditate on the Creator. Your eyes will see, tongues will speak and you ears will bring awareness. Your feet will bring movement and hands the ability to work and earn your way. Do not value the gift above the giver, for that is what the ego-driven do. All falsehood, secret and clever practices will be recorded. Those who are righteous will be exalted. They are enlightened and with the Wisdom of the Master, they will receive His Grace.

Man has fire and hunger within but without the Master's Guidance, he will be shattered by illusion and doubt. God grant me the Wisdom to follow your Path, so that by your Grace, I may find liberation. Blessed is the woman of faith, who brings forth her children to grow in true devotion to His holy Name. Without eyes, you cannot see. Without ears, you cannot hear. Without feet, you cannot move. Without hands, you cannot work and without a tongue, you cannot speak. So too, without devotion to the Lord, you cannot be Blessed with eternal life. Open my eyes, ears and mind that I may come to know the Lord, God Almighty. I pray with all honesty and sincerity. For I am just your servant and without your Grace, I will be nothing. I Praise your holy Name and humbly thank you for all your Blessings.

May we find Grace through Prayer?

Winter brings the fear of frost and cold but those who are devoted to the Lord will be enveloped in His Warmth. They will be Blessed with the sight of the Lord. Under the Lord, the King's merits in holy company, His devotees are immune from all harm. The Lord will hold those devoted to Him in His Mighty arms and they will remain there forever. He has great compassion for those who fall at His feet in Praise. In the winter, they will find His door to eternal peace and joy open to them. When the New Year comes, all pride and ego will be gone. There will be no attraction to lust or avarice. You will walk the holy Path devoted to His Name. You will bathe in the dust of His feet and with His Grace, find peaceful rest. All kindness, compassion and charitable deeds toward His living creations, will be counted. He will unite His devotees to Him. For those who meditate and sacrifice for the Lord, will be united with Him. As the seasons change, your True Friend, the Almighty will manifest in you. Together in holy community, Praise him. Such union will bring great Joy and Bliss. Finding the fulfillment of a joyous Spouse, the heavenly choirs will sing celestial hymns in celebration. There is no equal to God. Nothing is like Him. He will Bless His devotees with eternal life, when they reach the Divine shore. You will be enlightened and be Judged pure, as you find yourself at His holy feet. This is the treasure that you will find when you have crossed the impassible ocean. You will be Blessed through your loving devotion. All months, weeks, days and moments will be melted, for there is no measure of them in eternal life.

I will be devoted day and night to the holy Preceptor. I will shed all

ego and seek His shelter. I will Praise Him with sweet words, for He is my True Friend. I will find comfort in Him for without Him, I am lost. I have searched the world and know that my actions and good deeds are what bring me God's Grace. Save me Lord, God and bestow your Grace on me. Save me from all sorrow and suffering. I pray in your holy Name. Enlighten my mind and come to lodge in my heart. May you hear my prayers, oh Lord. Bless me with your Love and everlasting life in your Divine Home.

Fill your heart with Truth and He will bestow His grace

Those, who are totally bound to illusion are drowned in duality. Their extravagant clothing and trinkets are of little value. The slaves of death will take them to oblivion. The ghost of man will turn their hair grey. They will reap what was sown in this world. Those protected by the Lord, who seek His shelter, will find refuge. Board the Ship that will cross the ocean of existence, guided and protected by the Lord. In the autumn, rise the waves of passion. This passion is the Love of the holy Name. The mind and body are yearning for the sight of the Lord, God. This thirst can only be quenched by the direction of the Mother and keeping holy company with those ardent in their devotion. Touch the feet of the disciple, who reminds you that without the Lord, there is no Joy. There is no shelter. Love comes from devotion to the Lord, God Almighty. They joy of such Love will bring fulfillment. Those who believe will be united with the Lord, renouncing all evil and ego. Attached to the scarf of the lord, we will attain union with Him. In the autumn, we will live joyfully, meditating on the holy Name and receiving His Grace. Autumn's message is simply that you reap what you have sown. There is no blame to any other. Forgetfulness of the Lord, brings only malady to the plant's roots. Worldly pleasures will automatically forfeit all intersession with the Lord. All complaints will be nullified, there will be no help for such. However, by Supreme good fortune, union with the Lord in possible. All alienation can be gone, if you join holy company. Anxiety will be relieved.

Union with the Lord, God Almighty can never be calculated. Cast

away all suffering, ego, torment and loneliness. Instead, find Bliss in His service, with your necklace of Pearls, Rubies and Diamonds of pure devotion to the Lord. All doubt will be annulled. In winter no fear will you have of the frost and cold. For the Lord will embrace you in warmth and Joy. Your devotion to the lotus feet of the Lord will bring many Blessings. You will be Blessed with the sight of the Lord and you will be safe in His protection. Through Praising the holy Name and service to the Lord, you will reap profit. You will be saved from all thoughts of materialism and doubt. By the mighty hand of God, you will be protected. For He is your True Friend and you will know His compassion. All desire will be controlled and through the Grace of God, you will know Joy and Bliss. In the dust of His feet, you will bathe with holy company and meditate on the Lord's name. You will be blessed with eternal life.

All ego and pride will be suppressed, all impurity washed away. Lust and avarice will not touch you, for you will walk the holy Path following His Will. You will serve the Lord and do good deeds and be honest and charitable. So then, the Lord will Bless you with enlightenment. Bliss will abound in you, through the Grace of God, and you will have perfect union with Him. All sorrow will be banished. The Divine King will be your eternal mate and choirs will sing Heavenly songs of Praise. He will Bless you in this life and the Next. From the ocean of this existence, you will be rescued and you will find everlasting refuge at His feet. For you truly and genuinely meditated on the Name of the Lord. So you will be judged worthy at the Golden Gate passing the impassible ocean, all duality and falsehood gone forever. You will have obtained unity with Him and will be filled with His truth and Grace eternally.

Reap what you Sow!

In summer the joyful woman attaches to the Lotus feet of the Lord. Her mind and heart filled with the truth of the Divine Name. She quenches her thirst in the pure juice of His Bliss. All falsehood and evil to her are like worthless ashes. In holy company she is filled with the beauty of the forests and grassy glades. Through the Grace of God, she finds union with the Most High. Remaining in holy company with her sisters, the summertime brings her a beautiful necklace of the Divine Name to wear close to her heart. As autumn comes, some are lead to illusion and duality and become ghost-like. They shed their beautiful hair for grey lifeless strings. In this life one reaps what they sow As the fall continues, those who seek shelter in the Lord will find refuge. The refuge ship will bring them safely across the wild ocean. They will be protected by the Master, the Savior of all. As the waves rise, the love of the Lord, also rises and you will unite with the Lord, Most High. This union will bring you to safety. There is no other shelter.

Renounce all evil, ego and duality and He will wrap you in His holy Scarf. You will never be alienated again. Live joyfully in His Grace. Only you are responsible for your actions. You will reap the fruit of your deeds. Never be neglectful of the master, for this is the root of destruction. Never turn to bitterness or worldly pleasure for that will never bring the Lord, God, into your life. You will find no Grace or Blessings in these actions. Seek the Truth and Joy that is the Almighty. This will eliminate all alienation from the Truth. By Supreme good fortune comes unity with Him. Join in holy company and cast away all anxiety. As winter

approaches, wrap yourself in the beauty of all who seek the One, True God. Keep holy company and Praise the truth and the holy Name every minute you can. Let the Joy of the Lord blossom in your mind and heart. You will cast away all torment, suffering and loneliness and find Bliss in service to God. With a necklace laden with the Pearls, Diamonds and Rubies of devotion to the Lord, you will be presented at the Door of His Divine Home. No Chill or frost will touch or harm those devoted to embracing the holy Name. Their hearts are filled with His lotus feet. They are Blessed with the sight of the Lord. Their service and good deeds in this world are all counted and recorded. They are protected from all of the poison of materialism. By the Supreme One's mighty arm are His devotees protected and will never again be separated. They will live in the Home of their True Friend, the Lord, God Almighty. For they sowed the seeds of devotion, meditation, good deeds and service to the Lord and will reap life everlasting.

Only the Almighty is everlasting!

Follow the Path of the Almighty, as you make your life's journey. Those contemplating the holy Name will be saved from blame and stigma, as will their family. Those lodging God in their hearts will never know the torments of pain and suffering. They will be Blessed with the beauty and peace that His presence brings. Keep holy company frequently, to garner the wealth of the Master's Truth. Worship at the feet of the Teacher and you will be Blessed. Those who meditate on the Lord, the True Hero, will have good fortune. Contemplating the Lord in your mind will bring a Joy that is known to true kings among men. Evil will not touch those who, with God's Grace, cross the river of life with good deeds and devotion. Know the true reward of this life and hold Him as your Beloved and you will find Eternal Bliss.

Cling to the scarf of Truth and you will be enlightened and saved. By repeated devotion to the holy One, all fear is cast away. There will be no regrets. All desire is fulfilled by serving the Master. He is the Sole Creator of all beings. Touch the dust of His feet and you will be purified. All sin and suffering will be abolished. Water, soil, air and fire are all created by Him. All creation are His alone. Peace and Joy come from Him. He will be the sole judge who will join His devotees in Blessed union with Him. So too, He will cast away all evil-doers who are egotists. Those who pass through this world without the Inspiration and the Truth will be destroyed. Never let us lose sight of Him. We may wander all four corners of the earth in many directions to find your shelter. Grant us the Grace to follow the Path you have set for us, that we will find union

with the Lord. We, who are as useless as a dry cow or a twig without water, will die, having produced no profit. Let my life have true worth, oh Lord! Grant us everlasting union with you, we pray. Manifest within us so we can have you as our true friend. We will take no pleasure in the materialism of this world with all the fake decorations. We meditate on your holy Name and with your Grace will be united with you forever.

In the Spring-time, we will seek the company of other devotees. As your soft rain touches the earth, all living things blossom in your forests and valleys. So too, we will grow in our devotion to the Truth and the holy Name. We seek your Blessings to live united with you, oh Lord. Never forget the Almighty. Follow His Will or you will be tormented. Those who yearn with an open heart to see the Lord will have their thirst quenched. They will not be abandoned, rather they will have tremendous good fortune and Bliss. Those holy disciples, who lead us in seeking devotion to the Beloved will be united with him. I fall at their feet in gratitude, for they have opened our hearts and minds to know that only the Almighty is everlasting.

Find union through the acceptance of the Word!

The Master's Word is the Way to finding the Lord, God. The ego-centered person cannot know this, as he is caught in duality and ignorance. Union comes at the will of God and He will take away all suffering and doubt. True greatness comes from devotion to the Name. One with faith in the Name finds Joy. Only those who accept the Most High into their hearts will find true fulfillment. One who contemplates the Immaculate One, realizes His Essence and is freed from the consequences of their earthly deeds, through suppressing their ego. They will be blessed in the Name of the Supreme One, in whom they are devoted. Those, who by their ego and duality remain attached, will never be rid of their evil deeds. Through Praising the Master's word, you will know that His is a Sacred Lake, where precious Pearls will be found, bringing enlightenment. Night and day bathe in these waters and shed all impurity and ego. Purity comes with Love and devotion. Surrounded by the Lake, all are safe and protected. No amount of bathing will bring purity to the egotist.

Those who find the wealth of the Jewel and listen to the Master's Word will be filled with Grace and become enlightened. The Creator cherishes all. Follow His Path and you will be blessed. The world is full of materialism and man is influenced by it. Only those who find the Truth, with the Grace of God, will be welcomed into His Divine home. The world is filled with lust and violence, and the cycle of birth and death, that brings suffering. But the world, also possesses, the sole Jewel of realization and illumination. The disciple who practices chastity and restraint, through meditation, will become pure and lodge the Master's

Word in his heart. Those enslaved with the delusion live a life full of regrets. They throw away the Blessings of this world and the next. Open your mind and heart, and by Divine Grace, you can lodge the Lord in your heart. He will be ever at your side and will protect you through the holy Word. With holy company, sing Praise to the Sole One, the holy Master. Do not waste your life soaked in ego and duality, for it will bring you endless pain and suffering. He, who created all, will guide the devoted into union with Him, through their acceptance of the holy Word.

He, alone is above all creation. He creates and UN-creates, at His Will. He, alone is ever pervasive. Those turning to Him in humility, will find glory. He has no recognizable form or features but with true devotion, one will come to know the merciful and gracious Lord of all. Those who seek Him, in devotion, will be Blessed. Crave devotion to the holy Name, Beloved Lord, let us chant Praise to you, so we may be united with you. Cleanse my tongue, that I may be worthy to Praise you and crave union with you and find Eternal Joy with you. The ego-centered man is wasted, like the gambler's bet. Greed is the center of his world and he will roam the earth chasing materialistic reward. Our fortune will be found in cherishing the Lord Almighty. All on this earth are your servants, oh Mighty One. We fall at your feet, for we know that you are our True wealth. You gave breath to all the creatures of this earth, you are most Bountiful. There is nothing that we can imagine that can equal your Greatness. Only those pleasing you will be liberated. Who can be liberated? Who can be illuminated? Who is the Truth is the scriptures?

Who is the Head of the household? Who is the One who renounces the earth? Who is joyful? Who has only sorrow? Who is devoted to Divine Praise? What Words will still the restless mind? What teaching bring Joy or sorrow? Those who listen to the Master's words are truly liberated! Those who accept the holy Word are illuminated! Those who heed the path are united! Those who solemnly meditate are filled with Joy. Meditate with true fervor. Never let Him out of your mind. Seek the company of others devoted to God. Keep the Lord close on your journey through this life. Never forsake His Will and risk being cast away! Those with the Lord, God in their hearts, have true radiant beauty. Worship at the feet of the Master. Contemplate the wealth of God's Name. We are all owned by the Creator. Meditate on His name. Know that He is the Hero that owns all of the earth. He is the One and Only, who confers all good fortune, Grace and Blessings.

Contemplate Truth and find union with the Lord!

Through the holy Word all doubt is erased. Everlasting Grace comes from the Almighty. May you be blessed with Divine Grace? Let me sacrifice that I may become absorbed in the holy Truth. The Bountiful Lord is the Ordained of forgiveness and will bring Divine realization to his devotees. Those contemplating the Heavenly Name will, through His Grace, find Eternal Peace. Through the Master's teachings, the Immaculate Name of the Lord is exalted. Let us chant Praise to the Beloved so we will find everlasting Joy and union with Him. Those who are gripped by evil and duality will be heavily taxed by the harshest of tax collectors. He will punish those who neglect the holy Name and make them account for every minute, with no exceptions. The self-centered woman resides in her parent's home, while forgetting the responsibilities of her own home. She will weep bitter tears from her neglectful ways, not even finding peace when sleeping. But the woman who is visiting her parent's home, still never neglects to provide care for her own home and family because she cherishes them. She will be blessed with His sight through Divine Grace. By the holy Word she will be united with the Lord and hold Him ever in her heart. Take anchor in the holy Word and know that from your Blessed birth, by holding God in your heart and remaining devoted to the holy Master, you will know the Joy and ecstasy of Love. Those who are enlightened, study scripture and Praise the Most High, will come to the Divine door to be judged. The Master is ever present and knows and understands everything.

Materialism and duality will destroy the mind and leave you roaming

the earth without restraint. The mind that is bathe in filth will roam in filth, ego-filled and possessed by excess rituals. Nothing occurs except through the Will of God. If a man is born and dies and never knows the holy Word, his life is wasted in evil and ego. The egotist, like a beggar dressed in fine clothing without bathing, will soon find that his clothing smells of his foul odor. Rare are those whose faith is in the Truth: They will find spontaneous Joy, through the Master's inspiration. May we be united with the Supreme One and serve Him with an open and pure heart. Through the inspiration of the Master, Praise the One Truth and express the inexpressible with beautiful language. Then the enlightened mind will find love of the Truth. Their hearts are filled with the holy Truth and they will never know sorrow or pain. Those who love the Truth will never live with any falsehood or evil. Night and day, they will meditate on the holy Name and never be pulled away from the Truth, for it is lodged deeply in their hearts. Those who are deluded will remain ever blind. Their ignorance brings only pain and suffering. God, alone brings us into union with Him. Through the Infinite Word, all doubt, evil and suffering are annulled. One finds true greatness in the holy Name and through Faith finds, also, True Bliss and Joy.

The Lord God inspires all devotion.

God inspires those who win His pleasure and find the good fortune that brings Joy and Bliss. Through the Master's Grace, the Lord will be lodged within you. Eternal freedom comes to those who spontaneously lodge the Lord in their mind and heart and will find blissful union with our Beloved God Almighty through devotion. From excess rituals, you will become filled with evil and duality drifting aimlessly throughout the universe. Wasted are all hypocrites who never find the inspiration of the holy Word. They will be condemned to suffer. Those, who through discipline and Divine grace, quell the restless mind, will come to Supreme Grace. If anyone engages in falsehood and evil, their reward will be worthless. They will be drowned in duality and all their family with them. By deception and deceit, they will be drowned in poison. Only those blessed to have true devotion and love of God, will lodge the holy Name in their minds and hearts. The Lord will annul all ego and will quench the thirst of His devotees with inexhaustible treasures.

Divine enlightenment will open your eyes and all darkness and doubt will be washed away. All ignorance will be replaced with the knowledge of the holy Word. Faith will bring you to the Divine door and you will be freed from the slavery of evil and falsehood. You will be devoted to praising the Lord, God Almighty. Day and night meditate on His Name. Without the Word, you will remain in darkness and blindly flounder over the earth. The Lord is everywhere, although invisible. He will be found through Grace and good fortune. Seek the Lord and lodge Him in your heart and you will be united with Him in His Divine home.

With the Master's guidance, sing and dance, in ecstasy. Those having the holy Word in their mind will know everlasting life. They will cross all the stormy oceans of this earth, and will through their devotion save all their people. Those who are enlightened find true greatness in devotion to the Lord, God Almighty. They will gain everlasting purity through meditation on the holy Name.

Nothing happens except through the Will of God. He will guide all of His devotees to climb the insurmountable. He can bring life back to the dead. Union with Him will bring everlasting Joy. He, the Lord God, is higher than any other being in existence. May we serve the Lord, Master of all inspiration with unbroken meditation? May the Lord, life of the universe, bountiful Master, lodge within our minds and hearts? By His Grace, may He abide in those of us, who remain eternally youthful, with His Blessings. Evil and good live, side by side, in all of us. They are a part of creation. Only with the Master's guidance, is peace and Joy found. In each, duality and ego lies, however, these possessions can be discarded, with the Light of the holy Word. This is like the lotus in bloom, it can only blossom with light. So too, can our hearts find everlasting Joy through the light that comes from the Master's guidance. Inside each of us is a mansion with great stores of Jewels. These Jewels are the Name and the Word of the Lord and can only be attained with the Master's guidance. The devotee trades solely on these Jewels, his profit is the Name everlasting. The Lord God, Himself is a storekeeper. He bestows the Jewels on God inspired merchants. The bliss of His Grace comes through devotion and meditation. Praise Him and lodge Him firmly in your heart!

God's Name, alone, will fill you with Grace.

Reflect on God and through the holy Word you will become enlightened. Endless study will not satisfy the mind. Burning desire will not open the mind. Any falsehood or duality will poison the mind. If you buy such poison, by this poison you will be overcome and it will consume you. Seek the Master's grace and you will come to realize the One and Only, Sole Supreme Being. Suppress all evil and duality and Truth will prevail. Fill yourself with God's Name and you will attain the Master's Grace. Search for the wisdom of the Lord and you will find everlasting life. With the Name of God firmly lodged in your mind and heart, you will never travel the earth in fear, lost. God is ever present, seek Him and He will lead you on the right Path. Cherishing evil and ego are wasted. They will not lead to the Master's Word. One suppressing evil and ego will spontaneously find Truth. Discard all materialism and seek only to Praise your Lord, God. Let Truth and the Master's Word be your devotion. You will be inspired and find True Joy with God's grace. Truth will prevail, it is steadfast and everlasting. Through the Blessing of the Lord, in wisdom, is Truth found. Those devoted to the holy Name are truly wise. Blessed is their endeavor. Pure is the holy Word. Pure the Master's lessons. Pure the light that penetrates all creation. Pure is the song of Divine Praise.

Find purity in meditation. Those lodging the Lord in their hearts are Blessed with true Joy. The Immaculate Lord, God is Praised through the Master's Word. Thus, all desire for any falsehood is destroyed and the mind and body made pure. Chant hymns of Praise, holy choirs

will be heard by the Lord. All impurity and ego will be washed away. The purified mind is filled with the Divine Word and like a string of beads, adds another precious pearl. Great fortune comes to all who are devoted to the holy Name. Their devotion to the Word will reflect as beauty from their glowing faces. By indulging in impure foods, the filth of ego and evil are multiplied; only suffering and pain will be gained by such excess. Only the pure will be Blessed by Divine Ordinance. Be a swan on the glass pond with others of pure mind and thoughts. See your pure reflection and meditate on God, the Almighty, and you will be ever radiant. Meditate day and night on the holy Word. Chant Praise to the Lord. Such a dance in the mind will strengthen your devotion. The music of the holy Word will cast away all ego and materialism. Let no ritual or falsehood steal your mind and bring you suffering. True devotion is from God alone. The rhythm on the Divine Word brings great rewards. Never mindlessly or hastily keep time to the music, for your mind will not be devoted to the Divine Word. Don't expect income or wealth from such a performance, as it is no longer devotion to the Master's Word but for self-indulgence. Ego and duality comes from such performance and only pain and suffering will be the reward.

One who meditates on the Master's Word, truly pleases God. One who is devoted is truly free. One controlling their senses becomes a master of discipline. Submit to the Master's teaching, this is the way to true devotion. Realization comes through devotion to the Master. Fall at His feet while meditating on the holy Name, Praise Him, and no suffering will come to you. Those neglecting the holy Word have no shelter or anchor. They will be lost, as a raven in a deserted cottage, all

alone and suffering. They will forfeit all in this world and the next. They can record books of their thoughts on evil and duality using volumes of paper and ink, but they will find no Joy. They indulge only in falsehood and that will be their compensation. Those with only vanity in their hearts will be cursed. Holy the pen and paper that will record the Truth that comes only from God's inspiration. By recording the truth, eternity will be realized. The Lord, God Almighty, Creator of the universe, sees all. Only by His Grace is one united to Him. In devotion to God's holy Name, His Grace is bestowed.

Meditate on the Lord and find everlasting Joy.

Meditate on the Lord and find everlasting Joy! Such meditation will bring sustenance. Shed all ego and you will find the Lord. Devotion to the Lord, Master of the universe, brings everlasting Joy. Good fortune will bring union with the holy Word. True devotees will not be touched by impurity and evil. They will not be harmed by any aggression against them. The blind ego will lead to suffering, through evil and falsehood. Suicide and murder will come to those who slander the Lord's devotees. Those who are devoted, will be safe and unconcerned for they know they are cherished by the Lord. The universe is a garden, we are the plants and the Lord, God Almighty, the Gardener. He tends to His beloved children and will let no malady or pain come to them. Trust in the Lord and you will know peace and Joy. He, alone, confers knowledge and purity. All Truth is held in the hearts of those devoted to the Lord. With the holy Name lodged firmly in your heart, no falsehood, ego or delusion can penetrate. Hold on to the immortal Word and meditate on His holy Name. You will be enlightened though God's truth and Grace. Day and night, chant the Name of the Lord. Give thanks and praise with all your mind and body. God's Will should be your best desire. Following His Path is your strength to avoiding all delusion. You will never wander the earth aimlessly if you follow the Divine Will and hold His true Word in your heart.

Lord you know who is good or worthless, at the day of judgment, may we be Blessed with Truth and absolute faith. Through devotion, Bless us with your everlasting Joy. Banish all hunger and fill us with your

bounty. Enlighten us, oh Lord, and we will be filled with Bliss. Our thirst will be quenched. Lord, we pray that we will taste the everlasting Joy that will bring us eternal Bliss. Bless our eyes and minds with the vision of eternal Truth. Lord, God almighty, you are the one and only Supreme Being. Nothing is unknown to you. Enlighten us that we will know the complete treasure of your Grace. We pledge our devotion to you; to your Immortal Name and your Path and your Will! Save us from all filth and duality, and let us be enlightened. Let us please you and find Truth. Let us praise you and find union with you. Through Divine Grace, lodge your truth in our hearts and minds. We will seek such truth and in holy company, we will learn more from the tongues of those Blessed to share your holy Word. Let us be united to you, we beseech you. Meditate on the Lord and find everlasting Joy.

The Lord God is always with us, let us Praise Him!

The Lord God is always with us, let us Praise Him. Let us never find ourselves in the dark like a worm crawling through tainted meats. Cleanse us from the filth. Let us serve you, oh Lord, so we may, through good fortune, find the wealth of your Name. Let us know you, Lord God Almighty so in the hereafter we will be judged worthy. We will serve the Lord in purity and He will judge our actions. In these pure actions we will Praise the Lord. Those with ego, who use all evil means and false currency, to transact their daily business, will be tainted and their reward will be pain and suffering. They are deluded and will wander the earth day and night and will never find comfort. The Lord is our most beloved. Let us heed the Master's teaching. True devotion to His Word comes from following His path. All rewards come to those who hold Him in their hearts and follow His guidance. Pilgrimages to holy places and rituals will increase pride in those who are lead by ego and duality. But those absorbed I the Lord will find purity and Joy.

Without the Lord, God Almighty in your mind and heart, you will only know darkness. Open you heart and Praise the Lord and He will bless you with the wealth of His holy Name, stamped there forever. Through devotion to His holy Name, you will know He is with you and within you. Greatness comes from being Blessed with His light. Those with pure minds and hearts in this life will be judged worthy to enter the Divine Home. Let not false scriptures and readings delude you. They will poison your mind with materialism. Open your heart that He may ever reside there. Repent for all sin and evil and find the discipline to suppress

all that is not God's holy Word. Those devoted to His Word will find everlasting Truth and union with the Lord. No amount of knowledge or years of studying will replace devotion to the Truth that is God Almighty. Chant Praise to Him and feel the ecstasy that real meditation on the Word brings. True freedom and enlightenment are found in the holy Name. The true devotee can visualize the creation and dissolution of the universe. The Lord will guide them in their devotion. By Divine command, the earth and water exist.

By Divine command, also fire and air. By Divine command, man can be forever Blessed. By Divine command, with devotion, life eternal is ours. Holy are those who bring truth and honesty to their business dealings. With unending devotion, they buy and gain truth and Truth is their earnings. Without investment, no gain can be realized. Without Truth, as your asset, all is lost. Those who follow His Word and cross the oceans of the world in His merchant ship, will find Treasure. They will bring all their family and friends safely through all storms to find union with the Lord. No delusion or ego will steal the Wealth of those devoted to following the Lord's Path. Listen to the Master's guidance and know the wealth of His Divine home. The Lord is always with us, let us Praise him!

Lord God, Let me not be deluded by materialism!

Lord God, let me not be deluded by materialism. There is only one God. By His grace, may we know the Jewel of His Name. Let us never forsake His Blessings for falsehood and materialism. Through Devine Grace, alone, will we come to know God. Live in fear of God and lodge His Word in your mind. Chant His Praise and you will receive the Grace of Joy and purity. The Lord is the Creator of all. Know this and you will follow His Path and you will find rest. Through meditation, you will never need to fear the Lord. Through His holy Word, you will cross the worldly oceans without harm. Evil, ego and ritual practices, will not guide you to safety and peace. With bad deeds and regret, you will drown. Open your mind and heart to His holy Word and follow the Path of Truth and you will be Blessed. Day and night Praise the Lord. When the tongue is filled with devotion to God, you will feel the fullness of God's love. Serve the Lord, God Almighty, and through His grace, you will know the true realization of faith. Sing out His Praise and you will find the door to His Eternal home.

The Lord is like a tree filled with fresh and luscious fruit. Feast in holy company on His fruit and you will never know hunger. Even one piece of His fruit, when shared in holy company, will purify your mind and open the door to His Devine Home. Cast away all ego and worthless rituals and through devotion, you will look into the mirror of the mind and find God's reflection. Tis mirror will never shatter or rust. A true devotee will use the Master's Word to sing Heavenly Hymns and with His guidance, will find union with God, the Almighty. All ego, evil and duality will

be consumed and the door of freedom and bounty will be opened to His Divine Home. Lodge the Lord in your mind and you will receive Supreme good fortune. You will be Blessed and become truly devoted to the Master's Word. One who has truth in all of his daily life and places truth in all of his business dealings will be rewarded with plenty.

Lord come into our hearts and minds, for we are yours. Let us know the Word! Let us serve God and live a life of Truth, with His Grace. All good deeds and charitable donations, made in His name, are from the Lord. All false pleasure is discarded and the Blessing of Joy and peace will fill the hearts of His devotees. The blind fool will roam the earth and will never know the joy of everlasting life. Blessed are all who, in holy company, chant hymns of Praise to the One Supreme Lord. Hold the Lord God as your most beloved. Know the treasure of His holy Word. Follow his true Path and Will. Lord God, let us not be deluded by materialism!

Through Devotion to God's Word, let Truth blossom

Through devotion to God's Word, let the Truth blossom. Let the Jewel of devotion to the truth become our worth. Those devoted to the Lord's truth, know the secret; like the goldsmith who can tell if he has real gold in his possession. Though we live in a world filled with impurity and evil, we, who praise Him, will be safe. Through His Grace, we will be united with the Lord. The Lord, God Almighty will instill the love of Truth in all who are devoted to Him. Truth will surround us. Our Beloved Lord will shield us from want, desire, sin and evil. Meditate on Him with love and He will be pleased and Bless us with the gift of Light. He will bring us to eternal life. Nothing can happen without God. Let us serve Him and meditate on God, for He has created and expunged all life. You alone, Lord God are the Creator. You can make and unmake all things. For the Lord, God knows all life. His capability is beyond our imagination. But through the Master's teachings, we come to know Him. Let us lodge the Lord's Word firmly within us. Realizing the Word, we can win the battle with our doubtful selves, casting away desire and evil and becoming one with the Lord.

Those with blind ego, are devoid of truth. Only by seeking God can we protect our home. Through the power of the holy Word, all that is evil will be erased. Serve the Lord, God in devotion and you will know His Truth. You will be Blessed to become united to Him in His Devine Home. With each step you take to live in truth, realization will blossom. Nothing is real but God. With His approval, all that we do is

God inspired through faith. Under His benevolent eye, we all receive our earthly tasks and will be united with Him through them. Sweet is the Master's Heavenly Word. Rare are those who are divinely inspired to taste it, through enlightenment, is this Supreme juice imbibed. Heavenly music will be heard playing at the door to His Devine home. Let us fall on our knees to Praise at the Master's holy feet. Remove all impurity from us. Holy Lord, through our devotion, feed our insatiable hunger for your holy Name, with your Grace. Through devotion to God's Word, Let the Truth blossom!

May we be forever in His Grace!

May we be forever in His Grace. With constant devotion, may we be blessed with a loving heart that welcomes the Lord. Let us sing His Praise and know the strength of union with the Lord. Let us be forever devoted to His holy Name. Night and day, meditate on the Lord, God Almighty. By the Grace of God, we know that He is the Supreme Being. The One, true God! Those who accept His holy Word, are blessed to enter the Devine Mansion. Open our hearts and minds, oh Lord, that we may understand your holy Teachings. Beloved cherisher of the humble, guide us to the understanding and beauty of your holy Word. Let us never have vanity and ego. Wash away all of our sins and suffering and bathe us in the Truth of the Master's word. On our last day, may we be exalted. For we have been devoted to your holy Name. Comfort us and lead us to liberation in your Everlasting Devine Home.

Oh Lord, God, Beloved Friend bless us with true realization of You. Let no falsehood, evil or duality ever separate your devotees from you. Let no woman forget who the true Lord is. Through her good deeds, Bless her with your forgiveness. Let her enter your Devine Home and know life everlasting. Let us meditate on the Beloved Lord and we will all know true freedom. Those devoted to the truth will be acknowledged by the Lord. He loves those devoted to Truth and will grant them everlasting Joy. Cast off all evil and ego and find eternal Joy. True light will shine through on those devoted to God. Reach deep into your heart and you will find the holy Name by Devine Grace. Holy is the Lord! Holy is His Wisdom!

Gone is all darkness when the Grace of God is bestowed on you. Meditate on the Name of the Lord, The Lord is Immaculate, All-Knowing, Infinite, and He will Bless His devotees. Chant the goodness of His Presence. He will bestow His Grace on all who Praise His holy Name. Those who place the Lord in their hearts are truly fortunate. The selfish bride who remains sleeping and disregards the needs of her Spouse will be abandoned, she will be cast out and will find no rest. Yet the bride who is devoted to her Beloved and heeds the Master's Word will find comfort in His home. She will know the Joy and peace that true devotion brings. All accounts of good deeds and service to the Master will be acknowledged. Through Devotion to the holy Name, comes enlightenment. Through Union with the Lord, God Almighty, comes Grace. Through service to the Master, comes Eternal Joy. May we be forever in His Grace!

Come brethren, let us Praise the Lord!

Come brethren, let us Praise the Lord. Night and day, let us sing praise to the Lord. Our devotion to the Lord, God Almighty, will save us from all suffering and pain. The Lord sends the rain that will quench our thirst and nourish the crops of the earth to feed us. He will guide us on the right Path, when we open our minds and hearts to heed His commands. The Lord will bestow true bliss and Grace on all those He cherishes. Let us seek His Grace by kneeling at His feet. Let us contemplate His holy Name with each and every breath we take. Let us fall to our knees knowing He, Alone is our Master. All Honor and Might is yours, oh Lord. You bestow merit where it belongs. Night and day, we meditate on your holy Name. The Infinite, Lord, God Almighty will open our eyes and mind to Him. Ever Immaculate, the Creator will show us the way and the light. Obey the Lord and Master to find the path to Joy and true Bliss. Lord, your Greatness and Might, are unlimited. Give us your Grace, as we meditate on your holy Name. Fill us with the Joy of the holy Word. Through devotion to you we will find good fortune and come to please you with our humble Praise. We open our hearts and welcome our God. He is the One, True Love who can fill our hearts. In holy company we will find joyful days and peaceful nights. All sin is washed away when we are devoted to praising you, oh Lord. Behold, inside and out, you will purify your cherished brethren. All fear and illusion will be wiped out and the Lord will be firmly lodged in the hearts of His cherished ones. The Lord, God Almighty, is the beginning and the end. Through His grace we will be forever united with Him.

Lord, Creator, you are the One and Only God. Nothing can exist without you. Shelter us and protect us from all that is evil, we beseech you. We will sing your Praise. In meditating on you holy Name, your servant will find Grace. Bless us with the wisdom to know and follow your path. We will come to know our destiny by obeying your Will. My Beloved Friend, never let us forget your Greatness and Benevolence for a single breath. In holy company, keep us safe as we cross the treacherous oceans of the earth. Bring us safely to your Devine Home. All lust, sin and delusion will be annulled and all desire fulfilled. Through His Grace, we will find Peace and Joy! Come brethren, let us meditate on His Name! Come brethren, let us kneel at His feet! Come brethren, Let us give thanks to the Lord! He, Alone, is All-holy, All-knowing! He, Alone, can grant us Blessings and Grace! Come Brethren, Let us Praise the Lord.

You are the Beloved Mighty Lord!

You are the Beloved Mighty Lord. You are our life. The tidings that are revealed to us give us shelter. You are the True Almighty Lord. In singing your Praise, we find true Joy and peace. Hearing your word, purity is found. Let us join the holy devotees and contemplate the Lord, God Almighty. Holy, holy, holy Lord, God Almighty, bestow on us your Grace. Enlighten us, so we may come to know you. Holy, holy, holy Lord, God Almighty, bless us with true Joy. Enlighten us, so we may be blessed in unity with you. The Devine that we contemplate, brings us Joy, Peace and tranquil Bliss. Oh Almighty God, grant us the Grace and bounty that we may be truly fulfilled. Holy is the Lord, God Almighty, Creator of the world. Holy is the Master's Grace that guides us to His Path. Holy is the meditation that crushes all suffering through Him. The noose of all evil is snapped through devotion to the Lord. All delusion and ego is erased through devotion to the Lord, God Almighty. Meditate on the Lord and all sin and suffering will be cleansed. Through contemplation of the Lord, God Almighty, all hearts desire is realized. There is no fear, only Joy, when you Praise the holy Name of the Lord.

God, you are the true Provider. Let us never forget your kindness and benevolence. Through meditation of your holy Name and devotion to your Word, your Grace is bestowed. Holy Creator, ever merciful God, cherish us and bring us into your light. You are the Beloved, Sovereign Ruler of all the universe. The Lord, God is compassionate to the humble. The Creator bestows Joy on His cherished devotees. Like a loving mother, He tends to the needs of His children bringing Joy and shielding them

from suffering and evil. May we meditate night and day so we know freedom from pain. Let the wilderness become a safe path, through His Grace. Cities of the world, where the Lord's Name is not contemplated, turn to ruins. The servant or pauper, with their single crust of bread, who meditates on the holy Name, will find peace. The evil-doers, with their luxurious feasts, that are not believers, will roam the earth aimlessly.

Shelter us, oh Lord. Cherish us and bring us joyful Bliss. Banish all evil and suffering, as we fall at your feet in Praise. The Devine Word is like a soft shower of rain that perfumes the earth with fragrant flowers. Let us thank the Lord, God Almighty, for hearing our prayers and bestowing His grace on us. You are the Beloved Mighty Lord!

Blessed be the Name of the Lord

Blessed be the Name of the Lord. Bless us with the Grace to know you. Blessed be the hour when your word is heard in our hearts. Blessed are those who's Praise has been heard. Blessed are those who are worthy to kiss the dust of the Lord's feet. In holy company, may we come to realize the Lord, as our Friend and Beloved. In holy company we are saved and all our sins forgiven, and our mind and heart made pure. Take your children's hands, that we may know your love and never lose your Grace. Lord we will praise your Name and all agony and suffering will be replaced with Joy. Sing praise to the Name Devine and you will be filled with the Grace of God. All cherished creations will know His merciful kindness and will be filled with Grace. The Lord blesses the trees, plants, flowers and grass with a new freshness. Through the Master's guidance, meditate with a pure heart. He is Mother, Father, Brother, Sister and Friend to all. There is no fear with Him held firmly in your heart. He is your shelter. We are all part of His creation and all happens at His will. We have no power. Only through devotion to the Lord will we find Bliss.

Sing out His Praise and you will be Graced with a joyful mind and heart. Such Hymns your choir will chant and you will come to Eternal Life. Seek desire, in holy company, to find the Lord, God Almighty. Wash away all ego, evil and illusion and open our minds and hearts as we meditate on your Greatness. Through dedication and desire, He will bless us with Bliss, Joy and Freedom. Know the peace that the holy Lord's Name brings, through His Grace. Glad tidings we will seek, through the Beloved's Name. You who know all things, shelter us, Lord, God Almighty,

from all evil and suffering. Cherish us that we may be enlightened and guided by you, our Gracious Master. Through His Devine order, we will receive the Grace that will bring us Joy, Peace, Tranquility and Bliss. Through His Devine Grace, we will come to Eternal Life. Holy is the Lord, holy His greatness. Meditate with true devotion and all ego, evil and illusion will be crushed. All chains of fear will be broken and in a moment all desire to know the Lord will be realized. Come beloved friends and holy brethren, let us sing Praise to the Lord, God Almighty. Together let us meditate on our Creator and He will Bless us with our heart's desire.

Let us serve the Lord, so we may know everlasting love. Our, always merciful, Creator will tenderly cherish His devotees, like a good mother loves her children. The Lord, God Almighty, watches over us day and night, never miss a single chance to Praise His Name. Even the lowest servant or pauper, who have only a stale crust of bread, through devotion to the Lord, will receive His grace. The wealthy, with their luxurious feasts, who have no devotion or faith, will be cast out to roam the earth. Bring us to your shelter, oh Lord. Banish all pain and suffering. Shield us from all the ocean's storms and bring us safely to your Devine home. Lord feed us and comfort us that we will be showered with Joy. All that we have is yours, our mind, body, heart and possessions. At your feet, we beseech you to hold us close, truly united to you forever. Blessed be the Name of the Lord!

Never leave us Almighty God!

Never leave us Almighty God. Bestow the gift of Grace on your devotees. Bless us that we may meditate night and day on you, our Supreme Bestower. Come into our minds and hearts, enlightening us with your Joy and Pleasure. All gifts come from you, Oh Lord. Joy, free thought, pleasure, warm bed, soft rain and cool breezes. Grant us the enlightenment to meditate on your holy Name. Give us breath that we may sing your praise. May we be obedient to your will and worship you in all we do. Let your devotees hold you close and find a lasting Friendship with you through meditation. You are our very life's breath. Cherish us that we may find peace and through your Grace, Joy everlasting. You are the ocean, we the fish, guide us that we may never thirst. We seek you with the yearning of a baby for their mother's milk. The pauper who finds wealth, knows Joy, so too, will we find pleasure and peace, with you in our hearts. As the oil lamp dispels darkness, as the Husband fulfils His beloved's hopes, so though union with Him brings Joy. So too, with your love, my heart is filled with Bliss. Your holy brethren have guided me to the path of the Lord. Their love of Him has inspired me. The Lord, God Almighty is ours and we, His servants.

Take away all suffering and bring us Joy. Purify us and grant us the Grace to lodge your Word in our hearts. Satisfy us, oh Lord, that our faith can never be shaken. Those who come to know and love you, Lord, are Blessed with great fortune. Through your guidance, Master, liberate us and bless us with the wealth of knowing you. In your care, those who seek you, will become enlightened. Let us worship at the Master's

feet. Bless us, our family and friends, that we will be purified. The Lord, Inaccessible, Unknowable, Infinite, Almighty God, we sing your Praise and seek your Grace. Open our eyes to the True sight of Him, Lord, God Almighty. Let us be part of the few who come to know you. Through your mercy, inspire us to chant your Praise. Sleeping, waking, rising, sitting, may we spend each and every moment lost in meditation. Wash away all sin and falsehood and make us pure. Replace all ego and evil with Joy. Beloved Lord, free your slaves, that we may be cherished by you and safely cross the ocean of the earth to find our Devine home. Master, you are the One, true Teacher. No fear or evil remain when shrouded in your Vail of forgiveness. You cut the bonds of slavery and made us your cherished servants. Your Will and command are a pleasure to your servants. In obeying your Will all Joy is found. You exalt your true servant like a precious pearl and he no longer is judged but will live in union with you forever.

All goodness comes from within, only the deluded seek it elsewhere. Through the Grace of God will righteousness be found. A lovely stream of Joy and peace will find its way to the heart of those devoted to the Lord. Night and day, they will meditate on His name. The wilted tree becomes lush and green through the Grace of God. So too, will the heart and mind be filled with the guidance of the Master. Such a heart will become united with Him. Meditate on Him with all your strength. May we come together to wash the feet of your enlightened brethren and through them, may our eyes be opened to become dedicated devotees. Let me walk with supremely fortunate holy company, who can open my eyes, with your Grace. Discarding all evil and ego, worldliness and delusion, we seek your Blessings. Never leave us Almighty God!

Grant us your Grace, Oh Lord!

Grant us your Grace, oh Lord! May we never wander the earth and search all corners of the world endlessly seeking you, Lord. Rituals and repeated exercises or many pilgrimages to holy sites will not bring us enlightenment. Only through devotion to the Lord will we receive His grace. Only He can grant us union with Him. Praise Him and seek the Joy and tranquility that He can bestow on His faithful. Meditate on the One, True, Supreme, Devine Being! Inaccessible, Unknowable, Merciful to all who search for Him, Lord, God almighty, Creator of the universe. Through guidance of the Master, the Lord will liberate you. Through guidance of the Master, the Lord will become your true Friend. Through guidance of the Master, you will come to know the compassion of the Lord. This will be how the Lord will become lodged in your mind and heart. You will have no need unmet, when you fall on your knees in praise of God. He, alone, will cast your destiny. You will be successful in all deeds with the guidance of the Master. You will follow His command! You will graciously receive all He bestows. The poor and the helpless all place their trust in Him.

The Beloved will guide us on our Path. Sing out His Devine Praise, so you will come to know Him. All deeds of the earth are His Will. Inaccessible, Unknowable, Infinite, Almighty God, open our hearts so we may fill our minds with Your Truth. Let us never forget You, Lord, for a single moment. Banish all evil and sorrow from your children, so through your compassion, we may be Blessed and your Name firmly placed in our hearts. You, Lord, All-knowing, wipe away all sin and grant

us your Grace. You, Lord, alone can relieve all suffering and pain. Grant us the Joy of union with you. In suffering and in Joy, we will meditate on your holy Name. Blessed be the moment when we are united with the Lord. Blessed are the eyes that He has opened. Blessed is the mind, purified from all illusion. Blessed are all who live the holy Word, through His Grace. In devotion, all Joy and pleasure is realized. The Truth of the One and Only God becomes our Faith. You, Lord are the Bestower, the Mighty, and the Judge of all deeds. Bless us with the dust of the feet of the holy, so that all evil, ego and doubt will be banished from our minds and hearts. Grant us your Grace, oh Lord!

Lord bring us to Your Devine Home!

Lord bring us to Your Devine Home. There, we will know peace and Joy. Brothers and sisters who are devoted to the Lord, God Almighty, share the holy Word, that others may quench their thirst and come to know the Lord as you do. Master, bless me with holy company who can guide me to You. May I never stumble in my devotion to You or doubt in any way your Will. May I find Truth and Grace in the holy Word. Beloved life of the universe, Your Name is sacred to us. Let us repeat it often in true devotion, holding you in our hearts, that we may become one in union with you. Bring Joy to those who seek to become devoted to your holy Name. Enlighten us, oh Lord, we beseech you. Hold us close as we open our hearts to you. Light the Path so we may find everlasting union with you. No ego or evil will touch those, who through His mercy, have been Blessed with the Lord's Truth.

I meditate on the holy Name of the lord. In holy company I seek enlightenment that I may invite the Lord, God, to dwell in my heart. Inaccessible, Unknowable, Infinite, Almighty God, grant me the true realization of You. I will seek to know You through holy company who hold you firmly in their hearts. I will bow to those who praise you and kneel at their feet to learn your holy Word. Heavenly truth I will learn from the Master. Open my mind and heart that I will be granted union with You by God's Grace. I meditate on your holy Name at every opportunity with your holy brethren. Beloved brothers and sisters, come praise Him together and we will find true unity with Him, our true Lord and benevolent Friend. Everywhere I look I will find the Lord, for He has

washed away all the blindness and Graced me with True sight. Your light shines through your disciples, touching each heart with your Heavenly Word. And so the Lord, God cherishes His servant, and the servant is Blessed with the beauty of the Beloved Lord. The servant through his faith, will live in the Devine Home of the One and only True Benefactor, Redeemer and Friend, the Lord God Almighty. Lord, may I never know an hour without you. Take away my blindness and give me sight to know you, Lord. May I always be your servant and never depart from you. Happiness comes in your service! Happiness comes when you are lodged in my heart! Happiness comes in knowing that, through you Grace, my thirst will be quenched! Abide within me, my God, that I will never know hunger. Fill me with you holy Word that I will know true peace. Realization of You comes through devotion. Bless me with all desire to be your devoted servant.

You are the true King! You are the one and only Judge who can drown away all tears and sadness and bestow Eternal Justice and Joy everlasting. Open my eyes and mind that bring me into your Devine Light. Sisters, sing hymns of Joy! Where the Beloved has blessed the bride with Bliss. Her home is filled with peace and happiness and the Groom is blessed with charm and Grace. This bride has great fortune and wisdom. She will know her Husband's favor. She is blessed with enlightenment and she will receive her Beloved's praise. This union is Blessed with everlasting Bliss. The Inaccessible, Unknowable, Infinite, Lord God Almighty, is her Bridegroom. Her love of Him is her true devotion. As you have with this devoted bride, Lord, bring us to your Devine Home.

Lord, God Almighty, be mine!

Lord, God Almighty, be mine! You are the Creator, the Sole Supreme One, and the Eternal revelation; without fear or animosity, all-knowing, Self-existent, made known to man only through God's Grace. My heart is dedicated to the Lord, the holy Name, and the Devine One! Through the Grace of good fortune, I meditate on your Devine Name. Bless me with attaining perfect meditation. By being part of the devoted brethren, may I learn to follow the True Path. Be my life Companion, oh Lord, live in me and bring me to life's everlasting wealth. The wealth of union with You, my Lord. Wipe away any tears or doubts, like my mother did in childhood. Lord, grant me the Grace of having You in my heart, as my Teacher and Friend. Lord, take my mind and body, that I may know only You, as the One True God! May I, through your Blessings, find a teacher to guide me along Your Path. I seek You with every breath. In holy company, I will meet my Beloved. In holy company, I will come to know Him. In holy company, I will find the Lord, God, who cherishes His helpless children. You are both Mother and Father to me, who guides me. This provides the Grace of union with You, as does the water to the lotus in bloom. Without You, I know only sorrow and pain. I will contemplate the goodness of my God and learn His Truth.

With His brethren, I will sing His Praise. I will cross the oceans of the earth safely knowing that my Beloved is with me. He brings me glad tidings, so I may follow the Master's Path. I will call out to Him, repeating His holy Name to cure any doubt or evil. God will free me from sin and grant me shelter. The Lord is the ocean and we are the fish, without water, we will find only death. Brothers, holy men, devotees and teachers, bring me the True Word that I may not hunger. Help fulfill my yearning to find union with God. My heart will blossom with the Lord stamped firmly within it, through His Grace. Let me never stumble and fall out of Your Grace. Beloved Lord, keep me in safe company and grant me union with You, that I may find eternal life. Lord, God Almighty, be mine!

May I find True realization through His Grace!

May I find True realization through His Grace. In the Name of God may I be blessed. A loving mother watches her child grow, not understanding that with each passing day, his life is waning. She foolishly embraces the child thinking he is hers alone. Never giving thought to Truth, she remains deluded. Cast away duality and ego, that you might avoid certain death. Praise God and seek His infinite Word and you will find Eternal Life. Cross the ocean of this world in His Company. There you will find the Devine grace that will, through devotion, awaken enlightenment that brings union with the Lord. Leave behind all delusion, and fear no evil or death, once He, God Almighty, is firmly lodged in your heart, you are blessed! Those who pilfer another's home, will find no peace on their judgment day. Those who are pious raise their voices in prayer: "Unite me to You, Beloved Lord. Grant me union with You. Embrace me that I may never stray or lose my devotion to You. May I never wander from the path of Truth and light. Grant me freedom. God you know all things. Through You, my Devine King, may I become a vessel of the wine of purity. Intoxicated with the holy Word. Let me be as an unborn child in the womb, free from all pride and ego. I fall at your feet and beseech You to guide me through all darkness and torment to Your Light."

Through contemplation of the Lord, good deeds and self-discipline, may I never fall from Thy Grace. May I never seek to know the darkness of ego or duality. Save me Lord from all the evils of the earth. May I never cast you from my heart? May I never think that lust, pride and

falsely acquired wealth, will bring me joy or peace. In lust or the pleasures of this world is found no life. Shower me with the waters of Your holy Word. Then will I know no regrets. Greed and worldly wealth will bring no pleasure and peace, only death and torment. 'There is no difference between Thee and me, or me and Thee' as the bracelet is made of gold and the wave on the ocean of water! Through self-discipline and control, you will come to know the Lord and the servant, and you will find both within! Seek God, and with the guidance of the holy Word, you will find True realization through His Grace!

Honor the holy Name, Lord God Almighty!

Honor the holy Name, Lord God Almighty! Supreme over all. The woman of evil ways can come with an impure heart, dressed in falsehood. She attempts to dominate her Lord. Should she acquiesce, to become obedient to the Master, the Lord will see the change. Then by His Grace, she becomes a good woman who surrenders, body and soul, to the Lord and becomes devoted to His holy Name. The woman holding the supreme holy Truth in her heart, knows there is only one God. He, alone will judge who has a pure or false heart. Those who praise the Lord and are righteous, will be rewarded! The fallen woman, whose thirst cannot be quenched, will be abandoned. The woman faithful to the holy Word will find a marriage blessed with Love and Bliss. Those who have only ego and arrogance will be chastised and rejected. Give thanks to the Lord who shows the way and truth to those humbly seeking Him. Invite Him into your heart and find the serenity His Grace brings. Everything is His Will and that wisdom is found only through devotion. God will absolve all sin for those who cast away all ego and falsehood. The true devotee has faith in Him, the all-knowing, Infinite God. He is just and righteous in His judgments. To those of faith who praise Him, there will be everlasting union with Him, the Beloved. Through God's Devine Grace, you will be enlightened. You will know His greatness, find peace and become His cherished servant.

Evil-doers and slanderers are mistaken, for they will be alienated and know no peace. Good deeds, self-discipline and contemplation of His holy Word, will shed His Grace on you. His power is great. Just as He

can turn a crow to a swan, so too, He can turn the repentant sinner into a Faithful servant. Become His, body and soul, and you will become pure and radiant. Call out to the Lord, as a minstrel, and make Him your pillar of Faith. Gracious Lord, hear your servant! Be bountiful in your blessings, that I may meditate on the holy Word, and by your will, honor the holy Name – Lord God Almighty!

Freedom comes through God, alone!

Freedom comes through God, alone. He is the benefactor of all peace and Joy! Praise Him and seek His guidance in all things every day. Those truly devoted to the Lord will know Bliss everlasting. Hold Him firmly in your heart. By serving the Lord, you will gain honor and wisdom. Through praise of God, the Almighty, all ego and worldliness will be taken away and you will find enlightenment. All sorrow will be banished from you through your faithful devotion. He, alone, is the true Hero, who banishes all evil and demons. Sing out Praise to His Name to attain purity! End evil and duality with dedication to His Devine Word. Chant the holy Name of God and He will light your true path, liberating you from all that is false. See Him everywhere for He created all things. Through Him, all sinners can find Grace through devotion. Nothing happens without the Lord! He knows your every thought! He listens to your every plea. He answers your every prayer. Man struggles on earth until true realization come to him. If he gathers with holy brethren to Praise the Lord, his mind is purified. He finds peace in the holy Word and all darkness vanishes.

With each new dawn, he finds and accepts Him into his heart. Through obedience to His Word with self-discipline, solemnity and meditation, the Lord Grace's him with faith. On the Lord's Name, meditate! For He will quench your Thirst! On the Lord's Name, meditate! For He will feed your mind! On the Lord's Name, meditate! For He will guide you to eternal rest. On the Lord's Name, Meditate! For He will grant you everlasting Freedom!

With every breath may I praise the Lord!

With every breath, may I praise the Lord, my God. Let your heart and mind be saturated in the Love of God, the Almighty. Let your life be dedicated to the service of His Will. Sing out the holy Truth. Firmly lodge the Lord, God, in your heart. Hold tight the precious jewel of truth that will cleanse your mind and body. Forget all sorrow and delusion and fall in blind love with the Devine Spouse. In His love your faith will blossom. God is our sole Creator and Judge! Through devotion to Him you will have no fear. You will cross the ocean of worldliness secure in His care even while sleeping. Open your heart and become blessed with purity. Seek to remain close in your Husband's protective arms, so you may know true Bliss. Indelible is the love of God in the pure heart. Cross all continents and seas knowing He is your Protection and Hope. Live the Word of God and you will know His love. Earthly wares will not last, cast them aside and sail this world seeking only the Jewels of Truth and the holy Word. The secrets of the heart of all mankind are known to God. Those who follow His Path through righteousness will find Blossoming Joy through His Grace. Great is the Lord's Praise – Sing out His name! Great is the Lord's Praise – Know His Justice!

Great is the Lord's Praise – All good deeds rewarded! Great is the Lord's Praise – Never violating His Word! Great is the Lord's Praise – Conferring the gift of grace not sought! Bless me with understanding and self-control. Bless me with the wisdom to follow your will. For you are my One, True God and I, your devoted servant. No ego or evil, will I know, for He is in my heart. No unworthy deeds or thoughts will hurt

me, for His truth is my Destiny. In honest humility, I fall at His feet, and pray for a pure heart and knowledge of my God. You, my God, are the fisherman, let me seek to be protected by your net. No death will come to me, for I am enlightened by Your Grace. I will gather with holy brethren that I may be devoted to worthy deeds and Praise to Your holy Name. Lord, let me not be consumed by worldliness! Lord, let me not tend toward falsehood and evil! Lord, let me not seek pleasure that is not of Thee! Cast away all sin from me. Bestow the Grace of Your holy Name, firmly lodged in my mind and heart. With my every breath, may I seek to Praise You, my Lord, God!

Contemplate the Lord

Contemplate the Lord, know that He is your Beloved Friend. Those who meditate on the Lord's Name find a forever Friend and their heart and mind will be filled with peace and joy. God prevails over all land and sea, you will never come to any harm for He is watching over those devoted to Him. Board His ship for safe voyage with no doubt or suffering. The ship's goods are true devotion to the Lord Almighty and the Grace of Faith. Gather holy brethren and sail together in Praise of His holy Name. You will become enlightened and abide in his Devine home. In loving devotion, join the choir and with one voice, Praise Him. Let this be a pure source of finding His Blessing. Learn to find fulfillment in the will of God. Open your heart to offer lodging to the Beloved; thereby finding refuge and peace.

Be not deprived of True devotion to the Lord, for you will be as a fish out of water gasping for breath. Instead, in holy company, chant hymns of praise to Him. This will fill your heart and mind with a full desire to know the Lord. Not for an instant, can those who truly follow His Word be lost. For He is a benevolent Father who protects His family. Though you may cross the raging ocean, you will never lose faith in Him, for He is your protection and Teacher. Immerse yourself in Devine wealth, open your mind and body to Him. Indulge your heart in true love for Him. Firmly devoted to the Lord chant loudly with your holy brethren in True contemplation! There, you will find shelter and be blessed with eternal union with the Lord. He, Alone, is the Creator! He, Alone, grants all Grace! He, Alone, lights the way to eternity! In His Devine Name, I place my trust! In His Devine Name, I seek peace and joy! Through His Devine Grace, May I find Life everlasting in union with Him.

Meditate the Lord

Meditate on the Lord. Fulfill your heart's desire. Satisfy your thirst to know The Almighty. Serve Him and cling to Him and receive the blessing of placing Him forever in your heart and mind. Live in the temple of His truth. Humbly touch the feet of those who praise Him. Gently walk the earth knowing the peace of His Grace. Never hurt your fellow man but together sing His praise. The Lord, God, Almighty will speak through you if you are devoted to His Will… Be a champion of the Lord, forgetting all worldliness and folly by pursuing the treasure of Faith. In the stages of life, Man is born in naked shame, showered with a mother's love, then denies the Lord to seek the wealth and pleasures of youth. Righteousness forgotten, God's Will ignored. Eyes and ears closed tight do not admit the holy Truth nor taste the bounty of His Joy.

In your dimming years, take time to meditate on His Name. Do not regard worldly possessions with any great value. The son is held close by the parents, knowing he will provide for them in their old age. However, the true wealth is in seeking His Grace to follow His Will. Forget such earthly things and devote yourself to Him. Praise Him, follow His Will! As night falls on you, contemplate the Lord. In your final hours meditate every moment on His Name. Cast away all evil and ego, cling to God and beg His Grace, so you will be blessed with Eternal life in His Devine home. Dear Lord, bless me with enlightenment that I may truly follow Your Will. Shedding all darkness and falsehood, take me as your spouse, that I may make my eternal home with You in Joyful Bliss. Immaculate Lord, through meditation in my parent's home, I have come to know

You. By keeping company with holy brethren, I have learned to Praise Thee. Take me as your bride, that I may know the wedded bliss in your home forever. Be always my Beloved Friend that I may be swaddled in your immortal guidance. Through such union, everlasting Bliss and Joy is found.

Nothing can be achieved without the Almighty

Nothing can be achieved without the Almighty. No amount of study can bring enlightenment without God's Grace! Only through true devotion and faith in the Lord, can you be blessed with enlightenment. The Lord is found in His holy Word. Joy and peace come from true emersion in devotion to God's Word. Those absorbed with impromptu Praise of God are blessed with serenity and joy. The Holy Word is lodged firmly in the hearts of those who know God and seek eternal shelter in the Devine Home. Follow His Word to find that purity of devotion. Leave aside all ego and evil, to find honor and union with God. Your acceptance of the Invisible will lead you to the wealth of enlightenment, Faith and union with God, the Almighty. Praise His holy Name and find eternal happiness with the Father. The suffering of birth and death in this world will be forever gone. Live the Word of the Lord and follow His holy Will to become blessed with His Light.

Cross the ocean of the world with His compass to find everlasting peace and bliss. There is only ONE God! Seek Him in all those who know Him. Serve the Lord through good deeds and devotion. Gather in the Holy company of those who also seek to praise His holy Name. Absorb yourself in the Holy Word and find honor that comes from dispelling all ego and delusion, to open your heart and mind to Him. Those who know God speak only truth and through His blessing of wisdom will share and preach the Word of God. Enter the ship of Truth and find your way through the worldly waters to everlasting freedom. Though one may be alienated from friends and family, and fall to the

depths of despair and misfortune, by putting trust in God and seeking His Grace, he will find everlasting peace in His Devine Home. God is your real strength! All maladies of this world will be dispelled through praising His Name. Although a man may sin, and wander the earth in all directions, once he opens his heart and finds the true word, he will be blessed with forgiveness and everlasting peace. In one fleeting moment of true devotion to God, he will be saved. No amount of worldly wealth and rituals will bring eternal Light. Those involved in unscrupulous practices, for gain in this world, will never find true wealth. There are no rituals, disguises, penance, foods, celibacy or vigils that will bring enlightenment without His grace! There is no measure of His greatness! The Creator of the universe is immeasurable. Find Him in all creation. Praise His Name and follow His Will. The woman in a cursed marriage, abandoned by her Husband, will wander the earth in agony and pain. Should she beg to join the sisters who follow His holy Word and banish all evil and ego, she will be blessed with the Grace of God. She will be welcomed back to her Husband's home and there she will find true Bliss and Joy!

The Almighty is found through Grace

The Lord God Almighty is found through Grace. You will never find the inspiration to become devoted to God without Him guiding you with His grace. Only through Him will you find union with Him. A life without God is worthless and meaningless worldly attachments are fleeting. God, Himself, is your true friend. He, alone, can chaperon you to the true path. Without Him you will never find shelter and peace. Welcome God into you into your heart and mind and you will be Blessed with life everlasting. Cast away all ego and attachment and through devotion to the holy Word, you will find peace and Joy. Those with ego and evil will renounce acceptance of the Lord. They will never know the treasury of Blessings he bestows on those devoted to Him. Join together with others truly dedicated to following His will and living the holy Word.

Become immersed in the Holy Name of God. Partake of the Joy and peace He bestows. Lodge Him firmly in your heart, so you may never know the emptiness and sorrow of the heathen who wanders the earth aimlessly. Praise Him, follow His Will, and you will, with His Blessings, know the Bliss of eternal life. God sees all things, you will never be widowed and alone, if you follow the path of Truth. You will know True Bliss and be united forever with Him. Seek His blessings through good and charitable deeds. Become absorbed in the Holy Word, and spontaneously praise His name. God will become the Beloved of true devotees who cherish His Name.

No evil will come to those who follow His Will and laud His Name.

No evil and duality will dare to enter where the Lord is lauded. No harm can ever come to those truly devoted to Him. No matter the ego and falsehood of the demon father, the son will be emancipated and set free through his own goodness and devotion. Welcome the Lord into your heart and contemplate His holy name. You will be freed from wandering the earth aimlessly. In holy company dedicate yourself to Him. You will be Blessed with the inspiration of Truth. You will be fulfilled, through His Grace, and the Lord will be forever lodged in your heart. His holy Word will unite you in Eternal Bliss in His Devine home.

All happens through the Will of God

All happens through the Will of God. Follow the Master's teachings and you will be united to God. Cherish the word of the Lord with your every breath. Throw away all ego, greed and pride. Be like the lotus that blooms in water but dies without it. So you will bloom with the true Guidance of the Almighty, like a fish needs water, so you need the Word of God. The Lord, alone, grants union or separation! Through following His Word you will be blessed. All is at His Will! The Almighty is immeasurably. True devotion will bring enlightenment. His name should be ever in your mind, never mindless for an instant. Those enveloped in the Truth are not disguised from Him. With absolute conviction, follow His Word. Don't allow ego to make you stray into blindness or be robbed of your union with God.

Do not be like the woman in a cursed marriage who becomes abandoned. The forsaken woman will forget her path and stray from her home, only to find suffering. However, if she decides to seek truth, she can once again be united with the Lord. Praise God and rid yourself of all ego with His grace. Through His Blessing alone will you come to know Him. Worship at the Master's feet and become content, no longer believing that worldly attachments will bring you joy. Freedom comes from finding the Lord's shelter. With God lodged firmly in your heart, all evil and falsehood gone, you will find union with Him. No amount of rituals or holy offerings can rid you of ego and pride. Only through the guidance of the Master will you reach the door of liberation. There is only one Creator! And by His Grace you will realize Truth. Truthful

living is put above all else. From devotion to the Lord is contentment and knowledge of the Devine revealed. Those devotees will be greeted at the Eternal door and welcomed.

The stately mansions with all their finery will be empty inside and will give no comfort. They are only worldly riches that will collapse with all who reside there reduced to ashes. They are built of ego, pride and duality and have no bounty. The man who thinks he owns his family and takes pride in the sight of his wife will find only sorrow. Those who place all their pride in material objects are lost and will suffer. True value and wealth are found within, and only by the grace of God can be realized, when the mind and heart is open to Him. Without water, neither the lotus nor fish can live, nor the infant without their mother's milk. The mountain may seem insurmountable and the ocean frightening, but through God's Grace nothing is impossible. Only the Lord God is Immortal. All that are born must die! All worldly wealth and earthly things will pass. Be not concerned with them. Hoarding gold and silver will not open the door to eternity. No elegant dresses, jewels or titles, will save those so inclined to ignore His holy Name. All will turn to ashes. This world is not everlasting. We are here to make a journey to our everlasting Home. No kings or statesmen or leaders of religion, will find access to Heaven. Only through seeking Him will the true devotee find his Devine Home, through God's Grace.

Live by the Teachings of Truth

Live by the Teachings of Truth, only then can you come to know the Lord. Joy comes from true realization of the Almighty. By bathing in the waters of Truth, you will make you mind and heart pure. There is only one Almighty God! The world is a magnificent creation of God. The moon, sun and stars have unique brilliance, they provide us with unlimited light. With true devotion, God will reveal Himself. With an open mind and heart, God will bestow the Gift of Enlightenment. With worldly desire and anxiety gone, Purity can be yours. No-one seeks pain, but looking for pleasure brings unending suffering. Let go of the ego and allow the Word to bring you Joy. Those who praise His Name will merit from His Grace. Those who neglect to Praise Him and wallow in evil-doing, will be left to wail and cry. By banishing evil and duplicity, you will open the door to Knowing Him. Fall at the Lord's feet and praise His Name. This will be your true wealth.

The Lord is your anchor, cling to Him. Those who do, though you are blind, He will bless you with Enlightenment. Those who do not search out the Truth, will be abandoned and filled with regret. They will be like the wayward wife who will never experience conjugal Bliss. There will be no room in the Devine home for her. Only through the holy Word, can she be united with her Heavenly Husband in His eternal Home. The true disciple casts away lust and ego to laud the Name of the Lord and cherish His presence in their heart. The wife who behaves offensively in the absence of her husband by wasting her beauty will find no bliss. With true devotion she will find her Husband's love and affection. The

wife who, by following the holy path and meditating on the Lord will find happiness and Joy. Life is but a fleeting moment. One who realizes the Holy Truth will defeat death and find union with the Lord. All who Praise Him with a pure heart will attain freedom from death and will live eternally in His Devine Home.

Only through the Word and teachings of the Master will you find Enlightenment. He is like a tree laden with fruit that also gives shade to those searching for it. The fruit will feed your mind and heart with the True knowledge of Him and His shade will shield you from all evil when you chant His Name with reverence. The Jewels and Pearls of His Devine wisdom are the real treasure. Find this Devine wealth through adoration to His Immaculate Name. The ocean of this world is daunting and without Him, as your compass, it is impossible to navigate. Cast off all ego and greed to serve the Lord and you will be enveloped in a blossoming love through His guidance. Be drawn to God like a fish to water and He will quench your thirst with serenity and joy.

Let God, alone, live within you!

Let God, alone, live within you. Find honor through His Devine name. Wherever you look find Him. The fish not heading the net, in the vast ocean, becomes ensnared by thoughtless actions. So too, will man, without guidance of the Father, find death. Swim instead in the Holy Truth and cast away all duality and evil. Don't be food for the preying hawk or be allured by the evil hunter. Meditate on the Truth and put full faith in the Lord. For there you will find the joy of everlasting union with Him. Lodge Him firmly in your heart. Without His Guidance, there is no Light. His teachings will bring enlightenment. By devotion to the truth, there will be no death. God, the Father, is your true friend. Through that union, you will be exalted. Death will not come to those who put their trust in God. The false mind and tongue can only be cleansed by the water of the Holy Word.

Through God's grace comes purity. What Joy is there in ignorance? With her Beloved gone, what loneliness the wife feels. Like a fish in shallow water, she cries out! Being heard by the Beloved bestows His Grace on her! Those who meditate with their sisters will find beauty bathe in love as she praises Him. Dressed in the Word she finds Bliss. The woman with a false mind and evil path will find only torment. The Lord will abandon her. She, who is married to the Lord, will be cast away for her pursuit of contention and hostility. The wife that wins His pleasure is truly beautiful and will be forever united through the Master's Grace! Reciting Holy Scriptures, penance and charitable acts, without devotion is worthless. You real what you sow Submitting to doing good deeds and

devotion to following the Word of God, brings Joy!

The merchant, without capitol, flounders while running in all directions. Not realizing the riches he is searching for are in his home He becomes tormented. Should he return home and contemplate, day and night, on the True Jewel, he will find his wealth in Faith. He should trade only with merchants who are guided by the word of God. Keep Holy Company and let truth be your cushion. Faith will bring the light of the Infinite One. Truly beautiful is the woman who firmly holds her Beloved in her heart. She will find true wedded Bliss in her Lord's merits.

God is both Mother and Father

God is both Mother and Father to all who seek to win His favor through devotion. Trust in His bounty and enjoy the playful innocent banter of a child. Teach me how to win your favor, I beseech Thee, my God. Keep good company and together Praise Him. True enlightenment comes with God's Grace and man's good deeds. Destiny is pre-ordained. Freedom comes with the realization of knowing that God resides in your heart. He permeates all creation. Worship God and search for the inner light that will bring peace to those who are truly devoted. The Lord is the wishing well of joy. By His Holy Name, you will find true Bliss. Chant His Name, never missing a breath that Praises Him. Find everlasting repose in His Devine home. He, alone, decides what to give or take. His creations are unlimited. He sees all things and blesses those who please Him. No man can fathom His power. Whether one is a king or pauper, God knows all and treats all equally when they are truly devoted to Him.

By falsehood, true love cannot be attained. The woman who pleases the Almighty, will find true wedded bliss. Dressed in the Word of God, the good wife will be dedicated in mind and body to serve her beloved. God's true devotee will open her heart and be a staunch believer and will be eternally united with Him. Devotion her elegant wear! Truth her fine styled hair! Her necklace God's Name. The Word, her lighted home. Her beauty, her love of God. Do not waste your youth and beauty in darkness. Seek the Lord and become united through His Grace. Follow His Will! God is the ship by which any ocean can be calmed. The Holy Word, the safe guidance to shore. Those who have no fear of God, will

surly fear the dark ocean. Frown on all worldly concerns and duplicity. Throw out the ego and desire that blind you from the truth. Through sincere prayer, find your welcoming safe shore, the Devine Home! In your Father's Eternal Abode, live in everlasting peace.

God knows the Truth!

God knows the truth. He sees the devious mind and heart. He, alone, knows when man deceives, not just in his home but in all places he lives! Do not forget the truth and the Lord. For He knows your every movement and false heart. Meditate on the Lord of all Creation, this will bring you true Joy. Everything is His will! The Lord will relieve those who are just and true of all pain and suffering. But He will leave all those who are deceitful and devious roaming the earth, wrath in pain. Only God can bless all with radiance. Greed and pride must be discarded to realize His union. Give me the strength to live, my Lord, that I may, with true humility, be devoted to you. God, the Almighty, become my one and only true friend, for many who are evil could steal my pure heart and try to leave me empty. God's gifts are limitless. Shower me with your understanding and light. Be gone, all of man's worldly attractions and bring me the treasure of your Joy.

My God, to you I dedicate myself, mind, body and heart. I cherish knowing you, for you are my Savior. Give me shelter, oh Lord, that I may never feel abandoned. Many are false and neglectful of the Truth. Many never take time to praise You or they praise You in pretense, to be exalted by their friends and family. So many think of earthly wealth, jewels and possessions and neglect all true valuable treasure. Devotion to the Lord brings true gain and fortune. That fortune is dedication to the real Truth. Know your God and forget your ego. Praise the name of the Lord at every opportunity. YOU can not hide your sins from the Lord. You must fall on your knees and seek His forgiveness. Fulfill the vows made in His presence. Seek His grace to make your mind and body pure. Know the bliss of singing His Praise. The Lord, more valuable that any diamond, precious jewel or pearl, knows the value of your devotion. Those serving Him become His Beloved. Self-discipline and single-minded devotion, will bring true enlightenment. Be gone all of man's evil, worldly attractions and distrust, and bring me Your true noble happiness. With true devotion to my Lord, remove all evil and sin, send me the treasure of your Joy! My God, to you I dedicate myself, mind, body and heart. I cherish knowing you, for you are my Savior. Know the Bliss of singing His praise.

Without God, Life is nothing!

Without God, life is nothing. I will call on my Holy friends to help lead me to the path of the Lord. The name of God, the Almighty, is a priceless jewel. Only those devoted to God will see the true radiance. Those who never seek to know Him are truly lost. They will roam the earth with no purpose. Those who are truly devoted, who raise their voice in praise, will receive His Devine Grace. May I follow the Master's guidance to obtain His everlasting Joy. Those who utter a million ritual prayers will find no peace without His Grace. Blessed are those who are fortunate to become united with God. The forlorn woman who repeatedly seek the Lord and begs the holy brethren to guide her in seeking His path will be blessed with His Grace. She will become enlightened. Embark on the ship that sails with devotion to find Him. Don't wade in the murky waters of ego and delusion. In yearning to know the Lord, seek out those who are already blessed with the light and are radiant.

When you come to Him with humility, He will Bless you with His Truth. God will bless the humble with good fortune and understanding of His Devine Word. The Lord will unite with the pure of heart who are devoted to Him. The happy good wife will take compassion on all who are seeking the truth and will speak of the Jewel that is her God. The Lord is the Supreme Joy that the pure of heart will find when the seed is firmly planted. Those devoted to Him will reap the bounty of true Peace and they will be forever united with God. Man, wife and family, who through ego and arrogance find pleasure in worldly pastimes will find no rest. They will never be fortunate to now true Joy. Without devotion, they

will receive none of His Grace. Fine homes and worldly riches will leave you impoverished in the end. Those who follow His Path will be Blessed in union with God in His Devine Home. Keep holy company and never behave with arrogance and self- absorption. Never thoughtlessly spend time pampering yourself when you should be praying to have Him take lodging in your heart. Only God can save you. Don't let ignorance and worldly passion blind you. He knows all things. Follow His Will and be Blessed with eternal Joy. Meditate on the King of kings, fall at His feet and Praise Him. Seek shelter with Him and all pain and suffering will be banished.

He, alone, is your Lord and Master

Be not deluded by your family and relations. That will not lead you to everlasting Joy! The Lord God, alone, is your true friend and master. He is your everlasting Friend. Never be betrayed into thinking that ego is lost without God's Grace. He is bountiful and merciful. He will bless those devoted to His word. Those who keep Him ever in their mind and heart will know His Bliss. The pure mind and body will be united with the Lord and will find everlasting peace with Him. Rituals will not cast away ego. Do not be deceived! Only through following His Will and praising the Name of God, the Almighty, will you find true Bliss. No freedom is found except through belief in God. Cast away your ego and follow the Holy Word, accepting the Lord in your mind and heart. Seek to banish all ego and falsehood, and through the Guidance of the Creator you will find the right path to Truth. Lodge God firmly in your mind and heart, devoting your thoughts to His Holy Name. This is true wealth. Success comes from bearing witness to God! He is your sole support.

Contemplate on His holy Word and Name, and by His Grace, you will become enlightened! Service and devotion to Holy Name, will fill your heart with love of His Word. There is no joy living in an empty house, no matter how big and grand it may seem. Fill yourself with His Holy Word and you will never be alone. You will, through devotion, live forever in his Devine Mansion. Sow the seed of His Word in your heart and He will grow there and bring you great Joy. Allow the Word of God to be your inspiration. Proclaim His Truth and all suffering will be banished. Keep in the company of other Holy brethren, who cherish the Lord and He will bless you with everlasting peace. The inner light will bring you the vision of the Lord. Never let delusion and falsehood blind

you. Follow His guidance and no ill thoughts will come to you. God is your sole savior. Sing out His praise and cherish the love of His Name! This will be your True source of everlasting Bliss.

Meditate and chant His Praise and you will become intoxicated with His Devine Grace. Become enraptured in this light reality. Live in obedience to God's Will! The wife with poor qualities will be cast away from her husband. Her ego will throw her from God's truth. She will be left abandoned wandering the earth without enlightenment. Obey God's will and open your heart to Him. The woman without devotion will never know peace. Those gripped by worldly desire will be abandoned. All who are filled with pride will only find torment. Any wife without her spouse's love will never be freed of her ego, and will be left in darkness and forever unfulfilled. Blessed are those who receive His Grace and are dedicated to their spouse in mind and body. Without ego, they will have love in their home and the Lord in their heart. The happy, good wife finds bliss in her bridal bed. In her mind and heart, she will come to know God.

Without God there is no Grace. Give up your pride and idle talk. There is only one God. The man who spreads the Word of God and meditates on His Name will be forever united with the Lord. No amount of bathing will wash off the curse of impurity and ego. Rituals will not bring enlightenment. No devotion to God is possible with an impure mind. Self-pride and ritual prayer will not cast away the filthy ego. God alone knows who has true faith. He will bless them with His Devine Grace. Through His Grace all ego is forever shed. Seek the shelter of the Lord. Be you king or pauper, He will know who comes to Him with purity of heart, to seek His Blessings! Wealthy are you who know the Almighty.

Be enlightened through Devotion

Be enlightened through devotion to His Holy teaching. Cast out the ego that would reside in your mind and make you blind. Seek to shed your ignorance and spiritual blindness through devotion to God! Those who prefer falsehood and evil, although they read the Scriptures, will find no peace. For they will not have any of His Devine Grace. Those with Truth and purity in their hearts will be Blessed. They will repeat His Holy Name countless times and follow His Will, thus finding True Bliss. Service to God brings Bliss and fills the heart's greatest desire. Purify your mind and body and make your heart a Joyful lodging place for the Lord. In union with Him, as your Beloved, enjoy the fullness of His Grace. Serve the Almighty! Cast off the ego like an abandoned evil woman, whose husband will never enter her bed! She will never enter the Devine mansion, for she only believes in worldly things, like great wealth, gold and fine jewels. She needs to display her worth through earthly wealth and demeaning others. She will never know True Bliss. Meditate on the Lord and keep company with Holy brethren, who seek the One Joy of knowing Him. The Almighty!

Be devoted like the good wife who enjoys the bliss with her beloved through softness and modesty. Blessed are they, who together fervently hold God in their heart and home. For they will follow His Truth and enjoy a blissful welcome as they enter his Devine Mansion. A good and faithful wife devotes herself, body and soul, to her husband, in times of feast or famine. She must live a life that is enlightened and pure, so she can attain honor. She must accept the guidance and Will of the True

teacher! The wife who seeks to fill her purse will find no rest. She is duplicitous and evil and will know eternal agony. Only through God's guidance and Grace will she find rest. If she cannot find the Word of God, her life is worthless. Falsehood, evil and ego will come with an eternal price. Union with the Almighty is True wealth. This, the devoted servant, will find and they will have serenity. Their mind and heart, in purity, will find True Bliss. God knows everything! It is through Him alone that grace can be Bestowed. He knows, each and every one, who seeks Him and who is truly devoted in all their deeds. He will unite them through His Grace to become more devoted.

Do not be deluded by your friends and relatives, for they will not bring you to everlasting peace. Never brag that you have many friends, for you only need One. The Lord is that True friend, who guides you to cast off your ego! God is gracious and bountiful and bestows the Grace of knowing Him. He resides in the hearts of those who are truly devoted. Blessed are all those who seek Him, for through His Guidance, ego is banished and Bliss is found. With Him lodged firmly in your heart, call out to Him at every possible chance. For through His Grace, you will be forever united. Through God's Holy Word, you will find eternal peace. Through His Will, He can unite all who praise Him and are devoted. To find the Lord is to banish ego. Become absorbed without ego or delusion and know His True Joy!

Taste the Joy of the Lord

Taste the Joy of the Lord and you will find a Sacred Peace. This will quench your desire and give you the Grace to live in Celestial Bliss. All ego gone! Let your devotion to God blossom. Infuse your heart with the Almighty. Few in this world truly serve the Lord. Banish all ego and greed. Make a place for God to live in you. Discard all duplicity and evil, only then can you reside in the Devine Mansion for eternity. Be self-disciplined and charitable then, with God's Grace, you will become enlightened. Never have lust or deception in your heart. Chase away all treachery and replace it with the Holy Word. Devotion brings Devine light. Be united with God. In Him your destiny is recorded. Feed your hunger with the truth that our compassionate Master bestows. Listen to Holy Teachings and with a pure heart receive His wisdom with True devotion. Only then can you reside in the Devine Mansion. The pure of heart are Graced with Blessings. The Lord is very close. See Him in all who are devoted to singing His Praise. Those with Faith in God will live in everlasting peace, with His Devine Grace, when they depart this world.

Those with duplicity and falsehood in their hearts and minds will find no rest. Chant His holy Name. Sing His Praise. Eternity will be granted to all who are true to His Will and are vigilant in their devotion to God's Holy Name. Blessed are those who obey His Will, their beauty will shine in His Devine Mansion? Meditate on God's Name, be the True and Faithful one who holds Him in your heart. Be ever mindful of the company of hypocrites and liars. Keep your mind and body

pure, forgetting all ego, to Praise His Name. You will be blessed and never know failure. He is the Ocean of Bliss, ever guiding your ship to the safety of His truth. Meditate on His Name many times daily, thus purifying your mind. Through the Lord's Devine Grace, you will know the Holy path and be ever enlightened. Contemplate His Holy Word with a truly devoted heart. There is no ego or delusion when you are graced with God's Bliss. He will bring Joy to your heart and peace to your mind, when you are fervent in your Faith.

There will be no Doubt

There will be no doubt or suffering in those who are fervent in their belief in God. With guidance one will unite in the Lord. Nothing, even the most precious pearls and jewels, have any worth when compared to knowing God. Your honest wealth is being one with Him! Share the Devotion with other holy disciples. Keep company with those who follow the Master's Teachings and are enlightened by Him. All ego and desire diminish when the voice is raised in Praise of the Holy Word. Your deeds will be noted in the hereafter. No falsehood will gain you entry to the Devine Home. You will know no joy and will reap only pain. To those who live by the Devine Word and contemplate God, all suffering and pain will turn to Joy. Come all brethren, friends and family, let us Praise God and know the pleasure of His Devine Essence. The bride who follows her husband to His home and happily they will share everlasting Bliss with Him. Sow the seeds of good deeds, water them by His Devine Name, and cultivate your mind to reap a True Devotion to God. No evil weeds will find their way to your home. Father, son, wife, mother, know that your good deeds are seeds, Truth the soil's irrigation and Faith the cultivator. Pride and conceit have no beauty and know no peace. Meditate on the Almighty, follow the True path with your voice raised high in Praise of God. Hold Him in your heart. Seek His Grace through prayer throughout each and every day.

Cast away all falsehood, any hoarded wealth and worldly things, for they will not take you to His Magnificent Holy Garden. Fear only God, the Almighty that you may follow His will in everything you do daily.

Even the lowliest beggar, who may have sinned by falsely cheating and indulging in evil, can seek Him and raise his voice in Praise and become enlightened by His Grace. He is the All-knowing and Almighty. See Him in every creation of the world. God knows our every deed, good or evil. Seek to know and follow His commandments. Dedicate your life and all thoughts to the Lord your God. For He has bestowed on us all gifts, every plant, tree, leaf or fruit of the earth comes from Him. Man must seek His Grace and become Blessed with True Enlightenment. Delusion is a thief of the mind! Man must follow His Will. Quench the thirst of knowledge through Holy Scripture and Meditation. For what good is a lamp without oil? Thus with realization of God comes great Joy.

Cast away all illusion, ego and worldly desire and with God's Grace let your heart be filled with Devotion to Him, The Almighty God. Now, as the mind is absorbed with the Lord, you will find True Joy! Be not tempted by the evils of the world- Lust has no Joy but God's Love is a True Jewel. Pursue Guidance from the Master to realize that everything is God's Will. There is no other Power but Him. Sing out His Name and know True peace. Be obedient to Him and know the light of Truth. Once your Faith is found, you will never fall into darkness though His Grace and you will live in His Devine Home eternally.

The Lord God is in you!

The Lord God is in you! Seek to immerse yourself in Him through Devotion. Those who are not enlightened by Him are lost. They have only empty ego! Now is the time to be His disciple and become united with the Lord. With every breath you take, right to your last, make your journey through this world worthwhile. Quench your thirst through Scripture, interpret and share all knowledge of God with others who are also His disciples. Let the Master guide you and forsake all worldly accomplishments as false! Through His grace open your mind and heart to accept Him. Knowing the Lord and serving Him is a true Blessing! Banish all ego, avaricious and lure of worldly pleasures. Be ardent and zealous in Knowing Him! Meditate on His name and you will obtain the true joy and wealth of knowing Him. All good deeds and charity will be counted in His Devine Home. Never forsake Him for any worldly thoughts or actions. True wealth is found in God. Through the master, learn that Joy! Contemplate all His attributes that are countless with the Bliss of a young bride's anticipation her future. Cherish His presence in you as a great and precious jewel. Share that Joy of Him with others who are also seeking Him.

Find your beauty in His Grace

Find beauty in his Grace! No beauty does a bride bring her groom if she is devoid of His truth and Grace! Seek His merits through Devotion- He is your Master! The Lord is your Home. Ask for His guidance in finding His everlasting Truth! Climb to the top of His Castle with true Devotion and meditation – Celebrate His Devine Name! The Lord is your Ocean, Ship and Anchor! Join all brethren, Friends and Family praising His unblemished Might. Embrace each other for your homily to contemplate and celebrate the Lord Creator. Speak of obedience to His word and Will! Unending are his creations that, in His Truth are devoted. Wisdom comes from the fear of not knowing and accepting His Greatness! Give thanks for being saved and having knowledge of His truth. Let go of the ego that will surely kill your Faith. Be His servant and all anxiety and fear will flee from you! Seek His Bliss and He will bestow it freely on those who hold Him firmly in their hearts. The earth is but a playing field and His Devine Mansion is the True Home of everlasting contentment and peace!

Keep yourself in Holy Company – join the choir of devotion to His Greatness and the door to Him will open to you. There, you will find Truth, Beauty and Love! The wife who dons her fancy costumes, jewels and fragrance, shall never please Him, if her heart is void of His Truth. This proud display of worldliness is false and totally known to Him. This pride in herself and her belongings will bring her much distress on the day of her death. Only those with devotion to the Lord and Master can find favor through His Grace. The narcissist will not find peace without

shedding their superiority and begging for God's Grace! Vanity has no worth! Humbly seek to know His Word and learn to meditate on His Holy Name. Gad has given us Air- from Air comes Water –from Water all was created! Let all your senses be enlightened by His Truth! Open your mind and heart to welcome the Devine Light! Safe in His ship of Truth, sail as a disciple delving the Ocean with the Master's guidance to truly know the Almighty. He, Himself grants Union! Eternal Peace. Cast out your ego and become united with Him and know Him above all else. Surrender to Him your Self, mind and body, so you will be Blessed with the Wonder of knowing Him, your God!

Know God and Praise Him (2)

Greed is a Curse, Lies a deceitful Thief that leave you as a decaying corpse! Defamation of others is a war of mud-slinging and hate! Be Graceful and Noble in all your actions and deeds. Forget the grand mansions and jewels and seek, only, to live in the Lord. Those devoting their lives to God will find His favor. Pray for His Blessings of wisdom, honor and the True wealth of knowing Him. Without His Grace, you will not know God, the Almighty! Hold Him in your heart and be a dedicated disciple! Only then can you be judged worthy to be in His Devine Home! There, the true disciple, will find Eternal peace. A place to rest and feast! Bring Him your sorrow and pain and He will grace you with Joy and Peace! Never forsake the Lord for fleeting worldly pleasure! Drink of His vine and you will live in His Devine Mansion. There, you will find a multitude of Blessings in one Blessing, that is Him! Cast out all that is false and impure. Never let him leave your Self or life! Nothing in this world matters but what pleases Him! Banish all that is worldly! Become the scribe with a devoted pen, recording on the virtuous intellect, all that He has enlightened you with.

Sing of His everlasting and endless Greatness, so that when you are called to judgment, you will be exalted to eternal Joy and Happiness. There, you will be honored by holding Him with you and in you, by His grace! Do not waste your time with idleness, be you a ruler or a beggar, serve your God with passion and reap His gift of the everlasting hereafter! Cast away all doubt, never should you know the fear of darkness! Dine on the Bread of Devine Bliss. Refuse all that comes from a tainted larder.

Stand tall and sing Praise to His Name! Wear the gown of True thought, contentment and charity! Unsnap the belt of worldly pleasure! Do not let that destroy your Bliss. Aim to fill yourself with the arrow of is Merits. He is our Home and Family. Humbly seek His Grace to find eternal contentment in Him. He, alone, will know your wealth and standing. Devote yourself to Him. Open your heart and mind, use the Gifts bestowed on you to enrich your intellect and Glorify Him to all men with your most reverent and eloquent Hymn. Never leave His truth!

Know God and Praise Him

In the name of God, the Creator, our knowledge of Him is through the Teacher's Grace No mansions of jewels or great fragrance of precious spices or of any worldly beauty should proceed Devotion to the lord- There is nothing of any value without the presence of God- No beauty is worth the loss of Faith and Trust in Him Never allow his Name to stray from your thought and words! If you are a ruler of men and they bow to you, or you are a servant Be mindful that you must keep God, the Almighty in your thoughts AND HEART –Revere His Greatness lest you fall into sin and forget your faith-No matter how one is blest with intellect and worldly goods- he is worth nothing without God. You can write a million books or reach great wealth but if the but if you do not do His will, you are nothing! Do not forsake your God for worldly goods or pleasure-for on the day of passing, you will be accountable- No amount of mourning for you will change your destiny in the eye of your Almighty Judge-God cherishes all His creations and the lowliest servant who held Him sacred and is devoted to His name will be exalted in the hereafter!

Enlighten us, so we will find our Heavenly home, Oh Lord!

In your home, sing Devine Praise, Meditate on His Glorious Greatness, For He is there to shield those who cherish Him. Your home and family will benefit from His Joy and Grace! There is no limit to God's benevolence at times of need- the birth, the union(marriage) or death are all known to Him- God is there—Bid Him welcome in your Home and heart, so you will receive His welcome when you pass to His Heavenly home in unity. Cherish the Scriptures and teachings, share the joy and bliss of God and seek to be a true disciple amazed by the limitless beauty of the sun, moon, stars, Mountains, Valleys, fragrant flowers and all the creatures of the earth. All are His wondrous brilliance! You are the Light, my God, I seek and submit to Your Sacred Will! Unquenchable is my devotion! Cleanse me from my sins and worldly thoughts that I may be as diligent as a hummingbird in the quest to attain Your goodness in me. Let all call His Name and be absorbed in Glorifying God's Greatness. Let us not be lost to you 0h Lord! Strive to earn His Merit and Grace, so as to enjoy the next phase of life with Him! Give us the light of Your guidance in seeking to know You and be liberated of any doubt of Your Mystery and Supreme Goodness!

Sing Choirs of heaven and Earth

Oh God, our Supreme Teacher, who loves all creatures, give us your Grace that we might sing in chorus with the righteous and the Heavenly Angles. The wind (air), the babbling brook (water), the dancing flames (fire), the birds and all God's creations become a symphony to celebrate and praise Him. Men of virtue, charity and poise, learned men and heroes sing in choirs to show their devotion to His Eternal Greatness. He is now, always was and always will be our King of kings, that all must abide by His will –Proclaiming His might and true power beyond any human understanding—The most learned Stewart of His teachings, the solemn or most virtuous are nothing without His Grace! Never deny or forget our God, the Almighty- Call His name often, one hundred times one thousand times a day- He is there now and always will be – He will never die! Call the name of the Lord for He is benevolent and will bestow Gifts of Grace – unequaled and unmatched on those devoted to Him! Envelope us in Your shelter, my God, that we may not be cursed- Let us pray for True Faith and let us seek to quench our thirst for Him through devotion. Bless us with a Holy Congregation who cherish our God and seek to know Him! No family, friend or neighbor can sustain us.

Only God can provide us with the necessities for existence. Only God can give us life! Holy God, Creator, You alone are the Provider! Let us meditate and praise Him! The Lord is both Master and Servant! You know of all suffering, You provide peace and Joy to those devoted to You, My Lord and God! God blesses the wealthy who are charitable and the beggar who graciously pleads for alms- For He created all and He blesses

those who pray and speak His name with reverence. Where evil tries to touch the world, God sees and answers the pleas of those devoted to Him. The Lord God is always staunch, watching over His creation- All that happens is His will! All those united with God through meditation and prayer will attain joy-Those condemned are cast away! Pray and read the Holy Scriptures- meditate on the Great One! Sing out Earthly and Heavenly choir to praise Him!

Seek to know God through all that is good and true

By knowing Him and living His truth, there is no death, no suffering, and no sin Goodness and knowledge will empower you with bliss and true faith. Meditate to attain full understanding of God and universal religion with only clear vision and no deviation to any lesser paths. You can find freedom through your faith and you will never have to plead for Devine Grace or Blessings. The door will be open and you will feel a real welcoming and enlightenment! Meditate on the innumerable creations of God.—the beauty of the mountains, the rivers, oceans and streams that God created, together with every living creature great and small. Every single thing God created is good! We must pray and seek Him! Immerse yourself in prayer, devotion, worship, Holy Scripture and teachings to become a devoted disciple.

Be charitable and pure of heart. Never falter, follow the path of righteousness. Do not fall into the folly of thievery, dishonesty, violence or sin. Cleanse your body with water, wash away the dirt from your clothing. Pray to God to rid you of all evil and sin, trading it for good. He is merciful and forgiving. Cleanse your body and soul with purifying water. Immerse yourself in charity, compassion, Holy Teachings and prayer to ask God to bestow His goodness and grace on you and rid you of all evil! Praise Him, the Creator of all! Only He knows when His creation began - the day – the date – the season – the month – the year! No man or book can count His innumerable creations! He is more infinite than all the oceans! He is all-knowing! There is no measure of God – His qualities, His benevolence, His goodness, His bounty! Be mindful and grateful for all the Grace and Blessings He bestows. You cannot receive without gratitude – Do not deny His Gifts for He gives

them freely without expectation. He knows our needs.

God is almighty, the King of kings! He alone, can liberate man from sin and elevate us with His mystical Blessings. There is no intersession except through prayer and devotion to Him. Meditate and sing His praises. Cherish the thought of knowing Him. Only those who abide by His will and raise their voices in praise of His eternal greatness will come to know Him. He is the Creator, the Almighty. He is Eternal, having no beginning and no end – Immortal! Live in contentment and contemplation! Let mortality be your realization. Have faith in God and let not human frailty stand in the way of your spiritual fulfillment! Be enlightened and compassionate! Let God live in your heart, for He is our true Master! Through your deeds and actions, and His Devine Grace, comes your destiny! Praise to God, the Almighty, Eternal, Immortal, through all time! Together with His regents, the Creator, the Preserver and the Judge, He steers them to His will and commandments. Although the Creator remains invisible, He see their work! He watches over the universe! If a man could say the Lord's Name many hundreds and thousands of times, this will show his devotion to become one with Him! He lowest forms of life (God's creations) would imitate man's devotion to God, if they heard of Heaven's Glory. Man has no power to speak or be silent, to seek or to give, no life or death, Wealth or authority come from man. Nor does meditation, enlightenment, knowledge or understanding come from man. This comes from the Power of God alone! He created night and day, all seasons! Air, water, fire and earth! He created the place for all to become good and righteous! God sees all things and all creatures of the earth, He is the judge of all! He, through His Grace will give His approval to enter Heaven! Then it will be known, the False from the true, the good from the evil, only then will God's judgment be revealed!

The Supreme One

He is the Supreme One, The Creator of all. Eternal–No beginning–No End. He is forever–Our Creator of every single thing, Earth, Water, Moon, Sun, Man, Animal, Plant. He alone gives life, He alone takes life away! It is only by His Grace that All life is attained and sustained Those who truly accept and believe shall have His Grace and Blessings bestowed on them and will one day have the true joy of entering His House. To know Him is to be ever mindful of Him! Only He can bestow that Grace! Only He knows what Truth lies within! Only He can bestow Real Blessings that come from knowing Him! Without knowing Him, man can have no real spiritual worth! No amount of riches, jewels, fame or acclaim from many millions Are worth a grain of sand, if one does not know Him, without Him man is nobody, nothing. He alone gives Devine Grace! All things come from Him, And with Him and in Him being in your mind and heart always. Those who know Him and are Devoted to Him experience Bliss! Through accepting His Holy Word and Teachings and by being Devoted to Him. You will know Him, God, The Supreme One, The Almighty

Running wrong way

Religion was introduced to improve ourselves. Everybody knows that we can make mistakes, to protect ourselves we should be religious. We should love but we should not be lusty, we should get angry at our own mistakes but we should not try to be a police force to fix others. Greed is not a bad thing if we are not hurting anyone, yes, we should not allow anyone to hurt us either. Why not get greedy to be a nice person. We all are possessive, nothing wrong in that as long as we are respectfully possessing God given privileges. But it is not religious to fight for anything which is not ours. Attachment is not bad either, as long as we are attached with well-deserved attachments. Yes, we should be proud of ourselves, proud is not bad as long as our pride is not damaging anybody else's credibility. We should be religious but it is not religious to force others to believe in your religion. Discrimination is not religious anyways. We are running the wrong way, instead of improving ourselves we are trying to improve others. May God bless us.

Almighty creator power,
only one, in everyone.
Ultimate truthful power,
only one, in everyone.
Absolute creating power,
only one, in everyone.
Unseen unperceived God,
only one, in everyone.
Unborn existing authentic,
only one, in everyone.
Undisputed original actual,
only one, in everyone.

Only God was existing
before all creation, is true.
God is presently creating
all creation, that is true.
God will always be creating
creation, that is true.
God created all elements
for creation, that is true.
Only God was existing
before air and water is true.
God created earth sun
moon and mars that is true.

How big is God's grace?
we cannot even calculate?
Yes, we are wise enough,
no one close to ultimate.
How we can avoid wrong way,
how do we go right?
Just leave this on God,
just relax, no need to fight.
Everything happening His way,
totality in his order.
If we understand his order
then relax obey his order.

Day night, dark bright,
this land is created by God.
Raining drought, winter hot,
earth is created by lord.
Days weeks months year,
heat air water earth space.
Fish fowl animal human,
insect creeping plants base.
All known for what they do,
there fact is there act.
Creator creating creation,
as they act, they face react.

Early morning woke up
with supernatural feeling.
As there is some quite comfort
or is some healing.
Woke up with a feeling in mind
about lovely Lord.
What a night I found myself
so close to great God.
can't define softness
colorful and great obsession.
But was really sweet delicious
supernatural fashion.
I don't know how to say
but feels like heavenly fall.
So, content so obliged
what I was looking I got it all.

One and only one Almighty,
absolute truth His name.
The creator self-created
no one ells can be the same.
Invisible omnipresent
unbound power, hard to trace.
All elements for creation
are absolutely God's grace.
He was present before creation,
before the total base.
Only his highness behind,
every system and every case.

I am grateful to the great
so many times, every day.
He can make a man divine.
god can do it in his way.
If there are million moons,
suns mars and many stars.
Still we are in deep dark,
if no God, can't see very far.
Always keep Him in your mind,
He the one only kind.
Without him is Barren land,
no fruit no one can find.

Universe is His creation.
He created all his game.
His grace is gift for all,
he blessed with his name.
Running everything
sitting alone, in His dome.
You are giving you created,
willingly you pass on.
You are beginning and end,
all straight all bend.
You playing you are game,
gladly watching same.

He is wisdom he is wise.
he is sunset and sunrise.
Earth star mars true all,
brightness and their size.
Very truthful is this all,
your order is not surprise.
All truth is your praise,
security guaranty or gage.
Your praise is self-respect
most praiseworthy act.
Truthful people praise truth,
this ideology perfect.

Big God bigger his praise,
like God no one can raise.
Whole world is his home,
he is present in his dome.
Savior saves one and all,
whom he chose he will fall.
Some people simply funny,
every time talking money.
But it is not their choice,
who is there to listen voice?
We can pass or we can fail,
the almighty will prevail.

Scripture can guide us all,
lift us up won't let us fall.
Always truth prevail,
going through hell all who fail.
We don't know show us way,
only thing we can pray.
Whatever we get will receive,
your gift our achieve.
Your word is best for all,
in scripture we should believe.
Your presence congregation,
nothing left if you leave.

Millions of preachers,
scriptures, millions of listeners.
Millions of loopholes,
commissions, commissioners.
Millions of naked animals,
insects, SeaWorld, birds.
Millions of air pressers,
waterways, millions of nerds.
Millions of cool, millions of fires,
millions of minerals.
Millions of births every day,
millions of death funerals.
Millions of hungers
millions of foods for world to eat.
Millions of praises and advise,
bare footers and fleet.
Millions of close and millions far,
millions of homeless.
Who is managing all of this,
nobody knows or can guess?

Sights nature, music nature,
earth, sky, ocean, all nature.
Total super scripture nature,
thought philosophy nature.
Water food clothing nature,
love attachment also nature.
Colors, community's nature,
every kith and kin are nature.
Goodness, bad boys' nature,
all respect pride also nature.
Fire, air, water, earth, nature,
sand, soil, ash, dust nature.
His nature, He is creator,
pure, power, perfection nature.
Unbound, unlimited, nature,
total grace of God is nature.

Air flows in his order,
unaccounted rivers all in His order.
Fire burning in His order,
nature turning also in His order.
Rain cloud in His order,
role of religious king in His order.
Sun, moon in His order,
million billion trillion in His order.
Logical and logic in His order,
entire universe in His order.
King queen all in His order,
He is ordering and He is order.

With His grace we have grace,
His every word is His grace.
No one can give like Him.
His blessings are with His grace.
All who give up their ego,
they are blessed with His grace.
We must be truthful,
if really want to expect His grace.
His mars, his stars,
his earth and his space, he is the base.
All crops, weeds, all fruits, seeds,
he is running he is race.

To feed ourselves we are dancing all,
running hard we can fall.
Running kings' queens and hero,
might have million or zero.
Only God don't have greed,
worldly things He does not need.
Lerner learn the holy theme.
roof is there because of beam.
Someone happy someone sad,
some disappointed some glad.
As we wish we can dance,
serious sincere respectful romance.

This is mine that is mine,
bones are mine and fat is mine.
Newborn mine, dead was mine,
pale is mine and red mine.
My good work, my achievement,
my school, religion is mine.
My wisdom and my mistake,
sometime real sometime fake.
My possession my obsession,
house family and nation mine.
Will cool down, we are hot,
not our sequel not our thought.

Rivers hills and all other sight,
animal, birds and human might.
Creator created this all,
no one owns them, we don't have right.
No one owns earth sky;
He plays His play all his dark and light.
His creation He controls,
why we should have un-needed fight.
Darkness is darkness,
we can't change night and make it bright.
We all are looking good in air,
but almighty is the one holding kite.

Unaccounted goodness,
unaccounted good, all there they should.
Unaccounted great people,
their life purpose is to fight for good.
We don't do anything on our own,
He handles his way and he would.
All happening is prewritten,
He created all, the best way He could.
Rightful is only God, He is doing right,
He gives to those who should.
Those who don't understand,
they are wasting life and they would.

Tons of books we can read,
with testimonials certificates we lead.
We can make records of knowledge,
study all schools and college.
We can keep studding whole life,
whole family husband and wife.
Till last breath if we keep reading,
whole life we keep on speeding.
All we do is all in vain,
whatever is written, only that we will gain.
You can do it again and again.
we can't change luck with extra pain.

Those who are singing in praise,
god loves them, their every stage.
But those who don't appreciate,
poor, unlucky, that is their fate.
Those who don't count them anywhere,
those are the one He care.
Their simplicity is their upgrade,
their simple success simply made.
God is in everything he made,
that is a real ink which never fade.
Whatever He puts in, that will show,
seed god so that will grow.

Short-lived all king, short-lived rule,
short- lived all public all tool.
Short- lived glittering gold,
short- lived all those people who hold.
Short-lived beautiful cloths,
does not matter how much were sold.
Short-lived are both spouses,
does not matter who was much bold.
Short-lived love short-lived,
but they forgot god who is ever lived.
Short-lived sweet, short-lived taste,
except God all taste is waste.

We can call true, if someone is truthful,
who don't have dust of lie?
We can call true, who loves truth,
those who praise his earth sky.
We can call true, who knows trick,
ready to grow seed and not shay.
We can call true, who is truly trained,
who is courteous giving hand?
We can call true, who is aware,
who trust in god, with all he shares?
Truth is Madison, to get rid of bad,
happy all truthful are never sad.

Lier queen lusty king, public illiterate,
unhealthy situation sick slate.
Wrong doctor wrong Madison,
how someone tell them you are great.
If you are giving kilo and expecting ton,
probably you won't get none.
If you are going wrong way,
everyone will stay away, nothing to say.
If you gamble lottery, probably you will not hit,
big one you won't get.
Mostly you lose your bet, running after big,
you won't reach that is it.

We try our best, running hard,
but what will happen, knows only god.
No power no right, we can claim,
no one is at fault, we cannot blame.
Nobody can meditate if god don't want,
forcing for anything, we can't.
Whatever we know, is God's will,
He keep us running and He keep still.
Whenever we lost, He show the way,
we should walk that way He say.
Father always takes care of child;
father know what to get hot or mild.

Just water can do, that water can play,
we learn from what master say.
Life is a car we are driving every day,
if we won't break it, we don't pay.
If we run it smoothly, do not overspeed,
that is good driving, we need.
If we force speed, trying to overdo,
you will get caught, paying for deed.
If you like to sneak, someone will find,
citation you will face some kind.
If under influence law will make arrest,
then you can't drive until test.

Law is very must, law should prevail,
if you don't obey you won' get bail.
They are messing up who do not care,
this is nice stage, why they share.
We got the chance to live human life,
we should not waist it, it is not wise.
This is time to sow seed, for feature,
hungry can't live long, law of nature.
Does not matter how tall, big you are,
if you are not fruitful, you are a tar.
Sweet sophisticated people are best,
wherever they go, they are guest.

Too smart some people, like to play bluff,
some day will face more tuff.
Someday we will go, leaving everything,
everyone will go beggar or king.
As we will sow so shall we reap,
have to live with that, we can't sweep.
We have to pay for all action bad,
yes, we will repent, yes, we will get sad.
Merciful content people compassionate,
that good creation god did create.
Gold is always gold, it might be old,
always precious always could be sold.

It does not make you rich if you dress up great,
greatness is inside state.
You can be great by great deeds,
can't get any good by harvesting weeds.
We can't be clean only by taking shower,
we have to bloom to be flower.
We cannot teach with only talk;
we can't show way which we don't walk.
You want to teach swimming,
you have to swim some,
show it how come.
If you have respect and fear that is great,
the best state is fear of ultimate.

That place is great where congregation,
where their almighty information.
That place is worship place,
where there Almighty is in talk, He is the base.
My heart goes to those who are there,
those who singing Him, his prayer.
Praising almighty is appreciable move,
that is the best, and is best prove.
When we are student, then we learn,
without studying we cannot earn.
Who praise ultimate they are great,
going the right way very great state.

Vegetation is living, all grains are alive,
dead cannot grow, cannot survive.
Water is alive, creation is with water,
for all the creation, water is starter.
Nothing could be grown, if land is dead,
that is a fact man, not only said.
There is a life in every living wood,
worms could survive eating just wood.
Without the life, air can't blow,
and without the air there can't be show.
We are illiterate, if we do not know,
every seed is living, dead can't grow.

When power creates, it can do alone,
when person creates, it takes two.
God created man alone,
man and woman made thrown, but not alone.
Women gives birth, world is not man made,
woman is not a man's bone.
Man criticize woman, who gave birth to man,
father cannot do mother can.
Female is friend, female is wife,
ruler king is son of woman, woman is life.
Power, not a person is almighty alone,
he is only self-created, no thrown.

Comfort zone

A lot of comfort in his zone,
god's grace can do alone.
Get rid of worldly litigation,
his dome is best station.
Just trust in only one,
creator of earth mars and sun.
All wisdom is his advice,
all scriptures is his surprise.
All who have him in mind,
those ones are best kind.
I would like to go that way,
same way I should pray.

Very sweet is his treat,
that level no one can beat.
Pride quits if he is in mind,
sadness quits every kind.
He is in mind then no worry,
no enmity and no hurry.
He is in mind, nothing wrong, unfearful every song.
He is in mind is best state,
our feelings become great.
He is in mind, I am glad,
he is in mind, why to be sad.

He is in mind, best oblige,
he is in mind you get wise.
He is in mind, is meditation,
he is only classification.
He in mind, holly shower,
he in mind spiritual power.
He is in mind, very kind,
all of others then left behind.
With his grace we can say,
with his grace we can prey.
He in mind, those are great,
those are spiritual mate.

Best state with him in mind,
nothing ells is of this kind.
Thirst quencher is his name,
he is playing he is game.
Nothing wrong no devil deal,
under lord safe we feel.
He is in mind we are content,
cleans mind sent present.
His feeling makes you great,
that pleaser is ultimate.
We can feel him with his grace,
he is the top he is base.

When no other relation is helpful,
god is there to help.
When there is no alternative,
still god is there to help.
Very big somebody think,
can lose everything and shrink.
Bigger the king bigger the pain,
worst pain king can gain.
Worshipers are doing great,
power kingdom all in vain.
Richer the man bigger trouble,
all air in every bubble.

The best creation is human race,
with congregation base.
Congregation is good way,
together they sit together obey.
Those who say, don't have might,
they are absolutely right.
Those who obey in good and bad,
they can never be sad.
They feel rich with god's grace,
they feel they have a place.
Best way of worship is trust,
then no hunger and no thirst.

Those are great who appreciate,
God's grace is ultimate.
Best performance we can do,
truthfully remember true.
Best state of mind is where,
congregation is sitting there.
Best preaching is revealing,
meaningful symbolic dealing.
Best incentive is motivation,
inducement of his relation.
Best place is spiritual home,
nonmaterial, psychic dome.

Save Him in your mind man,
unedited positive yes you can.
Remember him who persuade,
feel like you are his shade.
We should remember creator,
designer, producer, inventor.
Remember him who give food,
always thank him hey dude.
Who gave you air to breath,
who give you water you need?
Who give you all you got,
remember Him in every thought?

Taking care, birth to end,
why you can't make him friend.
Who provided everything,
to appreciate you always sing?
Who is always omnipresent,
ubiquitous all over the tent?
Don't feel him away from you,
what he did no one can do.
Materialistic we are all,
consumerist bourgeois halfwit call.
We are running after fake,
but ever present we should take.

Why we play brute, beast,
we should be human at least.
We pretend wise and clean,
inside why we play so mean.
We can't sing without tone,
your wrong right all you own.
We want things to possess,
then you deal with your mess.
Enmity dissension opposition,
all this is our own creation.
Let us pray savior to save,
otherwise consequences grave.

Almighty God we can pray,
you save us from going away.
Without grace nothing can shine,
me myself nothing mine.
You are mother you are father;
we are all your child rather.
Console comfort and solace,
beyond compare your grace.
No one knows your height,
unbound and limitless might.
Only you know your truth,
your veracity your genuineness.

Prophet is the inspired lord,
proclaimer of the will of God.
Prophet is always uninvolved,
uninterested, unconcerned.
Some flower grows in mud,
looking good smelling instead.
Prophet never want to hurt, impair,
injure or incapacitate.
Like sunshine for everyone,
prejudice discrimination none.
Prophet is always submissive,
humble, meek unpersuasive.

Prophet always utmost pure,
unmixed occupation tenure.
Prophet has utmost knowledge,
grip on misgiving college.
Prophet don't have friend or foe,
proud, honorable show.
Prophet is utmost height,
but never like to show his might.
Prophet is blessing for all,
considering small but very tall.
Prophet utmost perfection,
complete combined no section.

Prophet is an utmost trust,
prophet always great, no rust.
Prophet always very kind,
that state of mind hard to find.
Prophet is son of prophet,
same position the same locket.
Prophet is alternative lord;
prophet is kind of present god.
Prophet can define prophet;
prophet know divine prophet.
Prophet is a present lord;
no doubt prophet is a living god.

Millions of people dedicated,
millions of people educated.
Millions of people searching god,
visiting forest jungle holt.
Millions are reading scripture,
millions sitting quite picture.
Millions are dumb inarticulate;
millions are speaking great.
Millions are running after money,
millions of playing funny.
They are doing as directed,
they are performing as selected.

All who feel they are too big,
their own grave going to dig.
All who feel they are too sweet;
they will get negative treat.
All who feel proud of wealth,
they are sick, is mental health.
Humble submissive with his grace,
fair course they will face.
Some possess rich and rare;
total will vanish evaporate in air.
Who is feeling too strong,
his tenderness emotion is wrong?

Who is feeling very kind,
his sentiment emotion is blind?
Who is feeling contributing,
into air subscribing shooting?
Who is content with what he got?
gratified is his thought?
With his grace you are obliged,
with his grace are advised.
He is playing he is the game;
he gives you; he is the name.
All truth is only one God,
other all fake complicated nod.

He is boundary and unbound,
he is listening he is sound.
He is creator but uncreated,
cosmopolitan, sophisticated.
He never born, never die,
but omnipresent on earth sky.
His creation never sees him,
he is in us; we never be him.
All the nature in his order,
he is recording he is recorder.
Running the world, he enjoys,
for him, we are all toys.

Invisible unseen undetectable,
blessed ones know label.
Hey man keep him in mind,
nothing there is of his kind.
Gave up all love lust,
unapparent closeness is very must.
We were made human kind,
to keep close him in mind.
Human race has one chance,
get involve in his romance.
He is always in our mind,
we should try yes, we can find.

Everything is in his hand;
he is listening he is the band.
He is growing he is growth;
he is taking and he is oath.
He created all creation;
creator have the information.
Any time he can make bend,
he started and he can end.
This is his choice to stay alone,
all will end what is shone.
He can choose to keep growing,
he can end all he showing.

Content

I Found truth, I found
hundred percent, I am content.
Truth is in word form,
that is what I found and I meant.
I found truth, I observed,
preaching learning is in word.
I found truth, with patience,
was welcomed on interns.
Song of joy all around,
very professional does it sound.
Sing just spiritual song I heard,
and that song is in word.

Hey you myself stay with god,
no pain if there is lord.
Read write listen lord,
without word we can't say god.
If you have great word,
everywhere you will be heard.
Save the word your savior,
great word can fix behavior.
God have all every game, every ball,
who gets is his call?
Who have his name he can sing;
god knows who is king?

His true name is my base,
nothing more I am content.
Nothing ells I need,
tranquility, peace calm is present.
God made me grateful,
appreciative, obliged thankful.
Love your word, respect your word,
you will be heard.
We have five senses, perception,
feeling in our word.
Lucky we, have sensation,
use word in worldly fashion.

Running wrong way mistake,
self-control what it takes.
We can control with gods will,
otherwise no good until.
No one ells can help,
With the grace of god help yourself.
True attachment with true name,
that is the real game.
If we have him cent present,
only then we feel content.
God could upgrade refine,
ameliorate, enhance outline.

What will happen is written,
it cannot be changed.
Take what you are blessed with,
can't be arranged.
Nothing could be changed,
with mischievous mind.
Disobedient not good, unruly,
wayward and errant.
How to find out his highness,
surrendering our self.
Just obey his order,
capitulating, giving up yourself.

Smart infrastructure won't work,
not in his dome.
Attachment, greed is elusion,
does not have home.
Possession, control,
custody always changing hand.
Stay with permanent,
who own all space and land?
Do not go that way,
do not do that you will repent.
Don't be ashamed of,
regret, grief disappointment.

Come one come all,
read scripture, not picture.
Lot of wisdom is written,
watch the spectacular.
There is lot of trash writing,
not worth reading.
If we are driving wrong way,
all in vain speeding.
Truth is a Dimond word,
always worth reading.
Candor veracity sincerity
genuine way of leading.

Can get advice in words,
we can get wise in words.
Can read truth in words,
can write truth in words.
Can sing praise in words,
can listen praise in words.
Can be named in words,
we can be blamed in words.
If you know to choose words,
you cannot lose words.
If you pick out right words,
don't need to fight words.

Creator of power is power,
order heat order shower.
His order he is obeying,
carrying out following power.
He is fact and he is finder;
he remembers his reminder.
He is fire he is the savior,
rescuer deliverer liberator.
He is life and he is living;
he is taking and he is giving.
Those who understand,
they are game, and are vining.

Author producer director actor,
is one and only one.
Wordsmith playwright dramatist,
one and only one.
Fabricator creator, maker builder,
one and only one.
Supervisor controller master,
also, one and only one.
Performer, player trouper,
is also one and only one.
Self-created one creator,
is part of all and everyone.

This feeling very healing,
palliate ease ameliorate.
Let us sing in appreciation,
cherishing, treasuring.
With this feeling this phase,
church worship place.
Revere, venerate, adore,
reverence prey to praise.
Using humble word trick,
Bow down before grace.
He hears you all the way,
he is building, he is base.

There was a reason
why god made this mankind.
We all have divine feeling,
but very few can find.
He gave us eyes to see,
we human are not blind.
But we watch fake world,
perishable humankind.
We greedy materialistic,
love lust we don't mind.
He is playing all this;
in every game he is behind.

He gave us power to listen,
we can listen truth.
Seriously, sincerely
with genuine, candor ruth.
Truthfulness sincerity
honesty is always great.
We are listening criticism
condemnation rate.
We can listen great word,
helping hand guide.
Authentic real true,
unadulterated bona fide.

Be content, listen content,
that is the only way.
Mollify satisfy, happy pleased,
yes, we can stay.
That is what, all we need,
we can get satisfied.
Human mission is
what to listen we can decide.
All listeners and all those
who are talking great.
Fulfilling human mission,
that state is ultimate.

Prayer

We are praying god for help,
only when we need.
But god is there to help us,
every minute in deed.
His activity performance
exploit action all the act.
Before birth we had that,
and always have in fact.
He is new and he is the old,
always will be there.
Animal human and fish bird,
just he is taking care.

No alternative for god,
replacement, substitute.
He is providing everything,
wonderful institute.
Always keep him in mind,
almighty is only kind.
Lord god is only one,
substitute you can't find.
No one ells are to pray,
what to ask what to say.
God is never overdue,
no one ells have any clue.

Short-lived all creation,
will die who are alive.
Five elements apart,
will dissolve senses five.
Short-lived all greed,
cupidity, rapacity a seed.
That will grow and go,
short-lived do you need?
Short-lived is anger,
attachment is short-lived.
Short-lived all you see,
proud, lust short-lived.

Scripture is The Master;
The Master is scripture.
True Master is the word,
Master is not a picture.
Anxious to see truthful,
apprehensive be truthful.
Uneasy and perturbed
disquieted worried fearful.
Master is melodious,
render quote speak reciting.
If melody is missing,
find truth in reading writing.

We want to be loved,
should become attractive.
Fearful respectful alluring
charming and effective.
Love is in yourself; you are love,
you are directive.
Get rid of anger greed,
lust proud you don't need.
Get rid of supplementary part,
get rid of all weed.
Volunteer to listen truth,
participate write, read.

How we can say and weight,
how we describe.
How we can put into words,
how can chronicle.
How we can be truthful,
how we can find great.
How we can sing in praise,
how to find ultimate.
How we report narrate
recount, or relate story.
How we can honor esteem,
himself is his glory.

Sun, moon, mars praying
in order are staying.
Flowers are perfume
scent all trees deodorant.
Air blows to keep cool,
with all tricks all tools.
What a devotion prayer,
activity fidelity rare.
Endless supreme sound,
unlimited, unbound.
God knows all the care,
in His order all prayer.

All of us let us pray,
just thank god we can say.
Appreciative we should be,
all we got is all free.
We fell in love with this world,
god unobserved.
Only who observe grace,
any pain he won't face.
All who born all will die,
that is the end of tale.
This is human exam,
learned passed rest will fail.

Where to go to find truth,
how to remind truth?
We should talk to truthful,
or walk with truthful.
How we should have to talk,
how should we walk?
Patiently we have to listen,
calmly walk to mission.
How to say what we seek,
stark open empty bleak?
Just listen nothing to say.
Truthful order just obeys.

How to get out of dark
dangerous way, safe stay?
As flower can bloom,
growing in mud, that way.
Where to find teacher,
where is the best preacher?
With his grace we can find,
should have trust blind.
How to find wrong and right,
what is dark and light?
Does not matter wrong right,
darkness never bright.

Who is happy and sad,
what to do to be glade?
All this is just a feeling,
every pain has healing.
We cannot stay alone;
we need someone own.
We all start from zero,
every Weak every hero.
What to do how we heal,
how ease soften feel.
Leave all this for the god,
he is living he is lord.

Without the grace of god,
actually, can't prey.
Where we will reach,
actually, we cannot say.
Without word how to teach,
no teach no reach.
Using word is all teaching,
in words is his name.
No word, nothing there,
in words is every fame.
All the world is word,
without word is no game.

Everyone is running hard,
to take money in hand.
Nobody gets satisfied
until graves mortuary band.
Nothing goes with us,
when people going to grave.
Money minded whole world
rich considered brave.
When we know we will go?
then why to make show.
Multimillion we made,
one cent, with us won't go.

God given at no cost,
each and everything we own.
God have unlimited treasure;
great giver is known.
For all that we got free;
yes, we should appreciate.
At least cherish, admire,
value, gift from ultimate.
Who is doing all that,
we should keep him in mind?
Doesn't matter how we take;
he is always very kind.

We are in trouble,
just because of our deeds.
Consciously, intentionally,
action we proceed.
Knowingly purposefully
we are running wrong.
All that what we listen
actually, this is our song.
Have to trust our creator,
kindly who did it all.
All this is his game,
he is playing and he is ball.

Blooming flower springtime,
if alone you are.
How you can live there,
how long and how for.
Firmament sky heaven,
beautiful atmosphere.
But we need love blessing
of the one who care.
Really soft, colorful,
really nice smelling great.
If you still crying there,
then that is your fate.

Manney prophet
prognosticator, utter divine.
Twisted tale bright pale,
all are good and fine.
Manney teaching preaching,
subject and field.
Manney sun moon star
Manney crop and yield.
Manney ocean hills rivers,
minerals and mettle.
Manney too smart people,
dumb driven cattle.

Manney king crown kingdom,
religion scripture.
Manney faith belief divinity,
theological picture.
Can't be cheated, deleted,
who believes ultimate?
Running around airing sound
always is too late.
All truth is just God, holiness,
sanctity sanctitude.
Very hard to describe,
all who try fastidious dude.

Control oven, patience cook,
recipe scripture.
Tolerance fortitude container,
stoicism fixture.
That is consoling food,
just blessed would eat.
With his grace win the race,
nobody can beat.
How we are performing,
all is being recorded.
What you sow, that you reap,
you get ordered.

How to keep close to God,
find grace of lord.
Check your words what you say,
how you pray.
Word is medium of exchange;
it is your range.
Your words are your view,
your words are you.
Your word can make, break,
just words it takes.
Word is your power,
curse or heavenly shower.

All this looks like mine,
all glittering is fake shine.
Nothing goes with soul;
we leave behind our role.
So why we do claim,
for our mistake who to blame.
Don't do the unfair, injustice,
deception is a shame.
Don't become wrong agent,
for that you will repent.
With his grace we can do
with his grace we find true.

Almighty created one,
and one created everyone.
Almighty created picture,
and started the scripture.
Almighty invented word,
and is wisdom observed.
Word is the first source,
word origin and the course.
Word is to write God,
to appreciate almighty lord.
Word is starting point,
pedigree and stream fount.

Virtue, ethical, morality,
virtue, goodness totality.
Virtuousness is the base;
virtuousness is the face.
Virtue is a grace of God,
virtue excellence of lord.
Worthless pride and anger,
love lust is all hunger.
Everybody knows this all,
but pride inside also tall.
We are searching all around,
inside us is unbound.

Human body is church,
every human has grace.
We feel him in there,
his existence every space.
Human body is best,
body home, human guest.
Only human can feel,
just human not the rest.
Greed is animal deed,
gentleness human need.
Humility is a process,
lucky who really proceed.

Where we prey is church,
we can feel him inside.
His grace we looking for,
he is guided he is guide.
There must be some reason,
human life is the best.
We will fail or get through;
human life is the test.
Very hard to pass that,
tough mission tough way.
Fake fraud hoax sham,
counterfeit could not stay.

He is giver, He gives satisfaction
and He is satisfied.
His grace is Bona fide
without deception he is guide.
He is the game, He is watching,
He starts, He is end.
He is prosses He is processor,
He get back, He send.
Billion Trillion years back,
just almighty was existing.
One and only one existing,
no picture and no fitting.

No component no accessory,
no day or dark night.
No sun no moon was there,
nothing shining bright.
No mineral no word yet,
neither water heat land air.
No consumer no production,
nobody visiting there.
No water no water canyon,
no ocean and no river.
No bad hell no good haven,
no month and no year.

Nothing to born nothing to die,
nobody passing by.
Nothing to teach, no teacher,
and was no earth sky.
No male female no cast creed,
no agreement, deed.
No motor or any vehicle,
no conveyance, no speed.
No sickness no cure,
Ayurvedic or no allopathy sure.
No religion no black white,
no rehabilitation restores.

No competition no fighting,
no hypocrisy no hope.
Pietism piousness sanctimony
does not have scope.
Creation was His choice,
no one ells had any voice.
His way, with His planning,
came up absolutely nice.
He created all the universe,
first of all, created heat.
Heat air water combine
created earth mars all fleet.